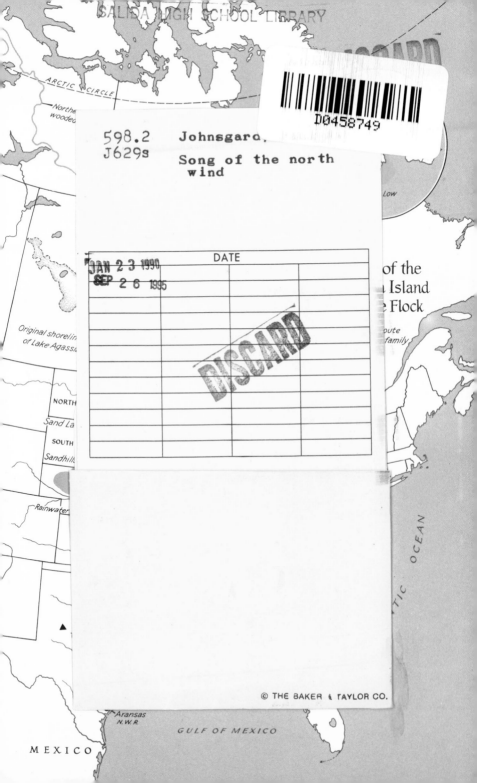

Song of the
North Wind

ANCHOR PRESS / DOUBLEDAY

GARDEN CITY, NEW YORK

1974

Song of the North Wind

A STORY OF THE SNOW GOOSE

PAUL A. JOHNSGARD

ILLUSTRATIONS BY

PAUL GERAGHTY

ISBN: 0-385-06785-2
Library of Congress Catalog Card Number 73–15348
Copyright © 1974 by Paul A. Johnsgard
All Rights Reserved
Printed in the United States of America
First Edition

To the memory of Black Elk (1863–1950),

his people, and their dream.

Contents

Song of the North Wind

Preface

For NEARLY SIX months the rivers and shallow marshes of eastern North Dakota are locked in the merciless grip of winter. By late March the snow begins to melt and flows into creeks and ditches that make their way to the Red River of the North. This river, which empties into Lake Winnipeg, drains the table-flat valley that once was the bottom of glacial Lake Agassiz. The Red River technically originates at an old Indian camping site once called Chahinkapa ("Opening in the Trees") and later named Wahpeton ("Dwellers Among the Leaves"). From this point, at the confluence of the Ottertail River, which has its origin in the glacial moraine of western Minnesota, and the Bois de Sioux, whose source is the northern overflow channel of Lake Traverse, the Red River flows north.

Lake Traverse, located just south of the point where the two Dakotas meet Minnesota, is the southernmost point on the drainage that collects the water flowing northward through the Red River Valley, finally reaching Hudson Bay. A few miles farther south is Big Stone Lake, the outlet of which flows into the Minnesota River, then into the Mississippi, and finally south into the Gulf of Mexico. Separating the lakes is a narrow valley floor that forms a drainage divide, the significance of which is overlooked by nearly everyone who travels the adjacent highways. Yet, the Traverse-Big Stone region marks not only a continental watershed boundary but also is the last area of extensive marshland south of the heavily cultivated Red River Valley. Furthermore, it is the halfway point on the 2,500-mile migration route of the snow geese between their Gulf Coast wintering grounds and their Hudson Bay nesting areas.

Lake Traverse represents a natural magnet for migrating water birds, which gain some protection from winter winds by the adjacent hills and find abundant food in the lake's shallows or in the nearby agricultural uplands. To this rendezvous each spring come hordes of canvasbacks and whistling swans, which after leaving their wintering grounds in Chesapeake Bay follow the valley of the Minnesota River northwestward across southern Minnesota. From the Gulf of Mexico come redheads, ruddy ducks, and lesser scaups; from the rivers and marshes of the Southern States and Mexico come green-winged teal, gadwalls, and common mergansers. For a few memorable weeks each year, between the end of March and the last week of April, these ducks and swans share Lake Traverse with one another and with the wild geese, forming a pantheon of waterfowl. Wild Canada geese are there, ranging from four-pound birds on their way to Baffin Island nesting grounds to ten- or twelve-pound "honkers" that will breed only a few hundred miles farther north. The watchful eye can also see white-fronted geese, which remain aloof from all the others and keep warily to the remotest parts of the lake. But the jewels of the lake are the snow geese.

By the first week of April the vanguards of the snow geese have arrived. Riding a south wind and a cloudless sky, they leave the broad valleys of the Missouri River not far from Sioux City. Under starry skies they fly northward, passing above the sacred red pipestone quarries of southwestern Minnesota, reaching Big Stone and Traverse lakes by dawn. Then, on tired wings, they snowflake downward into the waiting marsh at the north end of Lake Traverse.

As a boy growing up in Wahpeton, I measured my winters, not in terms of conventional time intervals, but in the days until the geese returned to Lake Traverse. By late March I could find scattered groups of mallards and pintails in thawing creeks near town, but it wasn't until the first haunting cries of the wild geese penetrated the evening air that schoolwork became drudgery and the only important event of the day was the weekend weather forecast. When Saturday finally came, the family car would be loaded with a change of clothes, a thermos or two, hip boots, binoculars and, when I had finally saved enough money to buy them, a camera and telephoto lens. Within a half hour I would be simultaneously jockeying the car through the muddy and badly rutted country roads of northern South Dakota and searching the horizon for flying geese. By midmorning the birds were headed back into the marsh after their morning foraging session in adjacent fields, and it was only a short time before the direction of their movements made apparent the best location to hide in order to intercept their flightlines.

This annual spring ritual of meeting the geese on their return from the south was more important to me than the opening day of the hunting season, the beginning of summer vacation, or even the arrival of Christmas. The spring return of the geese represented my epiphany, a manifestation of gods I could see, hear, and nearly touch as they streamed into the marsh a few feet above the tips of the cattails and phragmites. By evening I would be wet, cold, and exhausted from wading through icy waters and crawling through mud and snow. But during the drive home my ears would resound with the cries of the wild geese and, when I closed my eyes that night, I saw them still, their strong wings flashing in the sunlight, their immaculate bodies projected against the azure sky. They were my criterion of beauty, my definition of wildness, my vision of paradise. I had little idea of where they had come from and even less conception of where they were headed. I knew only that I must be there to see them, to become a vicarious part of something I couldn't begin to understand, but which to me represented the primordial energy of life.

CHAPTER I

Khavik and Khanguk

WE CAN ONLY surmise man's first encounter with the snow goose, but such conjecture may not be far from the truth. It might have occurred as recently as 10,000 years ago, or perhaps as early as 25,000 B.C. For a period of about 10,000 years, or until about 13,000 years ago, a broad causeway was open to land travel between Asia and northwestern North America in the form of the Bering land bridge. At that time, late in the last great glaciation, lowered ocean levels, associated with the massive volumes of water transformed into ice and snow, allowed the emergence of an extensive area of flatlands connecting the continental land masses of Asia and North America. Along this causeway came a variety of land mammals, including the first humans ever to set foot on the North American continent.

Perhaps they were a hunting party in search of caribou or other hoofed game. We can imagine them following the game trails, moving into increasingly unfamiliar terrain. A cold wind sweeps out of the north, carrying with it a curtain of snow that blots out the distant horizon and sometimes threatens to obscure their trail. Pulling their caribou skins closer to their bodies, they trudge onward, oblivious to everything except the trail immediately ahead. Then, from somewhere overhead, come the wild cries "Ka-ngok', Ka-ngok'." They look upward, but see only the low-hanging clouds and the approaching snowstorm. The calls become louder and, suddenly, below the leaden clouds, appears an undulating line of dazzlingly white-bodied and black-winged birds, pushing steadily eastward, the direction the men are going. The men stare silently at the alien birds, then at one another. It can only be interpreted as a favorable omen. In unspoken agreement, the men nod at one another and again move forward. The geese have now disappeared in the smoky skies, but man is about to set foot for the first time on a continent teeming with game, fish, and fowl.

The North American continent provided shelter and sustenance for these people ("Indians," as they were later called) who originally colonized it, and who gradually spread southward through the corridors along the mountains formed in the path of the retreating glacier. Much later the people arrived whom the Indians were to call "eaters of raw flesh" ("Askimek," later "Eskimo"), but who simply considered themselves as men ("Innuit"). They apparently crossed the Bering Strait by water and occupied the arctic regions north of timberline. Both groups of immigrants would live in peace and harmony with the snow goose. For the Indians the snow goose would symbolize the passing seasons, being too wary to capture or kill except under the most favorable circumstances. Its white feathers would be a symbol of the breath of life and a reminder of the intermediary role of birds as messengers between heaven and earth. For the Konkau of California, the snow goose became known as "God's bird," and they made beautiful robes from its down. For the Eskimos, the snow goose became important as a food source only, locally and seasonally, when eggs could be collected easily or where goslings and molting adults could be surrounded and driven into large stone corrals.

At the height of the last glacial period, ice covered most of North America north of the present Missouri and Ohio rivers. Paradoxically, some of the northerly parts of the continent remained ice free. These ice-free areas included the Bering land bridge and adjacent portions of Alaska and eastern Asia, much of Banks Island and the smaller islands to the north, and northernmost Greenland. One must imagine that on such areas the ancestral snow geese and other arctic waterfowl persisted and bred. Perhaps the white phase of the lesser snow goose survived in the region of the Bering land bridge, the blue-phase stock bred somewhere in the unglaciated parts of the Canadian Arctic

Archipelago, and the ancestral greater snow goose persisted in western Greenland. Presumably these groups wintered separately south of the glaciated areas.[1]

As millennia passed, the great glaciers receded and wasted away. At their leading edges massive lakes formed as the ice melted, inundating areas that only recently had received deposits of glacial till. The largest of these were the glacial lakes Agassiz and Ojibway-Barlow, forming to the southwest and south, respectively, of present-day Hudson Bay. Lake Ojibway-Barlow, the smaller of the two lakes, soon formed a drainage channel in the vicinity of the present-day Ottawa and St. Lawrence rivers. Lake Agassiz was destined to become much larger, and eventually did become the largest glacial lake in North America. Evidence of its presence spans 200,000 square miles, from northwestern Saskatchewan to northeastern South Dakota and central Ontario, although its surface area perhaps never exceeded 80,000 square miles at any one period.[2]

When Lake Agassiz first formed 12,000 years ago, the terrain surrounding it must have been tundralike, but pollen records indicate that a spruce forest soon developed along the lake's southern and eastern margins. A few thousand years later deciduous trees and prairie flora began to invade these areas. As the lake receded and finally drained into Hudson Bay over 7,000 years ago, grassland plants continued to flourish along its margins, and marshy vegetation probably developed widely over the areas of impeded drainage. In some areas these obstructed drainages resulted in lake-sized impoundments that remain to the present time, such as lakes Winnipeg, Manitoba, Winnipegosis, and Lake of the Woods. To what extent these marshes and lakes may once have served as breeding grounds for the snow goose and other waterfowl can only be guessed, but without question they must have provided the basis for the establishment of migratory traditions of arctic-breeding geese moving up through the Great Plains toward Hudson Bay.[3]

The Lake Agassiz region was important not only to waterfowl, but also to aboriginal man. Between the shorelines of Hudson Bay and the southernmost limits of Lake Agassiz lies a series of biotic regions, or "life zones," which reflect in space the biotic and cultural changes that occurred in time from a tundra-dominated arctic climate to a grassland-dominated temperate climate.

In the most arctic portions of the Agassiz region, in tundra adjacent to Hudson Bay, lived a group of Eskimos. Their culture was probably much like that typical of the other Eskimos who once lived across much of arctic Canada eastward to Baffin Island, and of the "caribou Eskimo" who still inhabit the region. In an Eskimo site (Thyazzi) not far from present-day Churchill, Manitoba, the small and finely chipped stone tools found suggest that their makers were predominantly caribou hunters, as are their modern descendants. The date of the Thyazzi site is tentatively 1500 B.C.[4]

In the transition zone between tundra and coniferous forest, Indians have lived for long periods, but little is known of their original culture. In a site (Duck Lake) in northwestern Manitoba some stone tools have been found, and limited evidence suggests a long-term tradition of big-game hunting, presumably for caribou. The modern Chipewyan cultures presumably derived from this hunting tradition.

The boreal forest has long supported an Indian culture of persistent duration and wide occurrence. A wide variety of small to fairly large projectile points found in a site (Grand Rapids) on the western shore of Lake Winnipeg suggests intermittent occupation of the area from about 2500 B.C. to the present. The Cree Indians are the present Indian occupants of the region, but they may have been intruders from elsewhere during the period of European contact.

A mixed coniferous, deciduous woodland-vegetation type connects the boreal forest with the northern grasslands. Indians living in these mixed woodlands during the "Manitoba" culture phase (A.D. 1000–1350) probably relied largely on river or lakeside food resources, such as fish, birds, and clams. An abundance of bird bones and small projectile points suggests the use of bow and arrow for bird hunting.

To the south, in the grasslands, a similar culture developed, but with greater emphasis on the hunting of large mammals, particularly bison. An earlier cultural phase (Whiteshell), extending back to about 1500 B.C., was also evidenced by rife bison bones and suggests reliance on big-game hunting in a grassland environment.

The grassland tradition of big-game hunting is probably far more ancient than is indicated by these finds. In eastern Colorado a "buffalo jump" dating back to about 6500 B.C. has been found, together with associated flint projectile points, suggesting that the Indians of the Great Plains were experts at trapping and killing bison long before horses entered their culture and enabled the Plains Indians to become the undisputed rulers of the grasslands. These tribes included the legendary warriors of the Dakotas ("Sioux"), Cheyenne, Arapaho, Crow, and Blackfoot, who were destined to rule the plains for as long as the bison trod the grasslands in uncounted millions. Only by exposing the Indians to his diseases and by relentless slaughter of the bison could the white man finally subjugate and eradicate the Plains Indians.[5]

Thus the pattern of land use and aboriginal cultures gradually developed in central North America, as witnessed over millennia by the snow geese on their annual flights to and from their breeding grounds in arctic Canada. To the Alaskan and Mackenzie Eskimos the snow goose is *kangok*, *kanguk*, *kuno*, *kagnok*, or other variants. By the Aivilikmiut Eskimos living north of Repulse Bay on the Melville Peninsula, the snow goose is called *khanguk*, the name also given it by the Okomiut Eskimos of Baffin Island. On Baffin Island the "blue" goose is called *kungovik*, while on Southampton Island it is usually referred to as *khavik*. All of these names refer to the birds' warning calls rather than specifically to their coloration. However, for convenience, the name *khavik* is applied in the text to the "blue" goose, while *khanguk* is used for white-plumaged birds.

Southampton Island, lying just south of the Arctic Circle, is the largest of the islands in Hudson Bay. It may be visualized as a gigantic goose flying southeasterly from the coast of Keewatin across Hudson Bay toward the Ungava Peninsula of Quebec. Its head at Seahorse Point is separated by some 200 miles from its tail at Cape Munn. A backbone of granite ridges arises at the eastern end of the island, and parallels the northern coast and adjoining Foxe Channel, rising to as high as nearly 2,000 feet. However, low and grassy tundra, interspersed with shallow lakes, forms the body and down-stretched wings of the goose. Cape Low marks the tip of one of the wings, while the other is formed by Cape Kendell. Between them is the Bay of God's Mercy, into which flows the Boas River.

The Boas River is named after Franz Boas, whose studies on the Central Eskimos of Baffin Island and northern Hudson Bay provide a major basis for current knowledge of this Eskimo group. According to Boas, one of the earliest contacts of the Southampton Islanders with Europeans occurred in 1824 during a short visit by Captain G. Lyon. Captain Lyon's group observed that the natives used limestone storehouses to keep their provisions of salmon, walrus, and seal, as well as carcasses of various waterfowl.[6]

Boas also summarized observations made by Captain George Comer in 1898. Comer found that the natives of the general area of western Hudson Bay were taller and their faces sharper than those of the more northerly Eskimo tribes, apparently a result of interbreeding with the Indians to the south. The Eskimos depended on caribou for food and clothing, using very few sea mammals. They also hunted musk oxen and foxes, and in the summer caught swans, loons, "brant ducks," and eiders in snares of fine strips of whalebone. In 1898 there were only 58 people living on Southampton Island, mostly on the Bay of God's Mercy. To support their huts they used whalebones, which were plentiful even though the whales themselves had become rare. They ate seals and walrus during seasons when the ice was strong enough to walk upon and caught fish by damming streams to trap them in pools, then spearing them. Wolves, caribou, hares, arctic foxes, and polar bears also inhabited the island.

However, a few years after Captain Comer's visit, all of the

Saglernmiut ("People of the Island of Saglern") were wiped out by an epidemic. Later, the island was repopulated by Eskimos from the mainland and Baffin Island, and the population grew. The caribou were exterminated in the 1930s. By 1930 the island supported 138 Eskimos as well as a few whites, mostly missionaries. "Civilization" had finally reached Southampton Island. In 1930 Dr. George Sutton also discovered that both snow geese and blue geese nested between the mouth of the Boas River and Cape Kendell and occasionally interbred, reopening the question of the taxonomic status of these birds.[7]

The recognition that "snow geese" and "blue geese" might not be distinct species was long in coming, and this delay has caused great confusion as to the proper scientific and vernacular names that might best be applied to these birds. Strangely enough, the relatively rarer and more geographically restricted blue goose was the first to be given an acceptable scientific name. In 1758 Carolus Linnaeus named it *Anas caerulescens*, basing it on an illustration published by George Edwards of a "blue-winged goose" from Hudson Bay. Eleven years later, Peter Pallas named the snow goose *Anser hyperboreus* ("goose from beyond the north wind"), on the basis of a specimen from northeastern Siberia. In 1822 Heinrich Boie proposed the generic name *Chen* to distinguish the blue and snow geese from the more typical "gray geese" of the genus *Anser*. Recognition of the existence of a larger type of snow goose, for which John Forster had proposed the name *nivalis* in 1772, was not fully established until 1927, when Frederic Kennard suggested the name *Chen atlantica* for the unusually large snow goose wintering along the Atlantic coast and breeding in northern Greenland. Similarly, John Cassin in 1861 described an unusually small form of snow goose as *Anser rossii*, using specimens sent to him by Bernard Ross from Great Slave Lake. These "Ross geese," or "horned wavies," had first been reported by Samuel Herne in 1770 from the Perry River area. Yet, not until 1938 were its nesting grounds finally discovered by Angus Gavin.

Of these four types of geese, the greatest taxonomic problem was posed by the blue goose, which differed from the "lesser" form of snow goose only in plumage traits. Its biological and taxonomic relationship to the lesser snow goose could not be established until its breeding grounds were located, which occurred after a prolonged search in 1929. Then J. Dewey Soper discovered the major Baffin Island nesting grounds of the blue goose. Although a few snow geese were also breeding in the area, he found no evidence of interbreeding. Therefore, he regarded the two forms as distinct species. Only a year later Dr. Sutton discovered the Southampton Island nesting population. Among 1,000 pairs of the two types at Cape Kendell, he found a few cases of mixed pairs and many birds whose appearance suggested that they were of hybrid origin. He considered that the two plumage types should be regarded as distinct, although closely related, species. In 1934, T. H. Manning visited the Boas River nesting ground and reported that about half of the total blue geese there were mated to white-plumaged birds. This percentage, he noted, was far below what might be expected if the two types were merely color phases of the same species, but at the same time he pointed out that few reasons could be marshaled for considering the birds separate species. He concluded that the relationships between them could be best expressed by regarding the two types as subspecies, a procedure that later was often adopted.[8]

The first person to suspect the truth was Franz Blaauw, an aviculturalist who bred snow and blue geese in captivity for more than 20 years. He found that crossing the two types produced offspring of either one parental type or the other, without intermediate or "hybrid" types of offspring. He suggested that the two types simply represent color phases of the same species. This explanation was amplified by Dr. Graham Cooch, who studied the Boas River colony for many years during the 1950s. He concluded that the plumage variations represent an example of adaptive polymorphism, the two plumage types having slightly different associated ecological adaptations, with different climatic conditions favoring one or the other. He also found that pairing between the two plumage types was common but

not random, presumably as a result of preferential pairing between birds of the same plumage type.[9]

Dr. Cooch also found that, in his study area, blue-phase birds
or mixed-phase pairings were reproductively more successful
than white-phase pairs, presumably because of minor ecological
differences in their nesting adaptations. Cooch concluded that
blue-phase geese were becoming more common in areas where
they had existed for some time, and also were moving into
breeding areas previously occupied only by white-phase ones.
In areas where such mixed populations occurred, the relative
rate of population increase of blue-phase geese was judged by
Cooch to be about one or two per cent per year. He reported
that by the late 1950s the incidence of blue-phase birds varied
from 50 to 57 per cent in three nesting colonies on Baffin Island,
from 30 to 35 per cent on Southampton Island colonies, 14 per
cent at Eskimo Point on the west coast of Hudson Bay, and
nearly zero along the arctic coasts and islands of the Northwest Territories.

In accepting the concept of a single species of medium-sized
snow goose, we must choose the earliest acceptable scientific
name for it. This name is *caerulescens*, which preceded *hyperboreus* by eleven years. The appropriate generic name might be
either *Anser*, if one believes this group of geese to be best considered part of the larger group of typical "gray" geese, or
Chen, if it is regarded as sufficiently different from the latter to
warrant special distinction. The former view is now increasingly
accepted, resulting in a single name (*Anser caerulescens caerulescens*) for both the lesser snow and blue geese. The greater
snow goose is now regarded as only a separate subspecies (*Anser
caerulescens atlantica*), while the tiny Ross goose is still generally considered to be a distinct species (*Anser rossii*).

The most recent population studies, by Dr. Cooch, Dr. Fred
Cooke, and their associates, have proven that the plumage differences between the snow and blue geese are an example of
genetic dimorphism and that the plumage differences are the result of the effects of a single gene, with the gene producing the

blue phase dominant over the white. Birds carrying both genes approach pure blue-phase plumage types, but usually have some white on the underparts. The tendency for birds to mate with those of their own plumage type, called assortative mating, has been established by Dr. Cooke's studies as the result of the goslings being "imprinted" on the plumage types of their parents, which is usually the same as their own.[10]

CHAPTER 2

Return to the Bay of God's Mercy

FOR MORE THAN eight months the life of the Arctic comes to a standstill as the land and waters bow to the elements. Polar bears wander aimlessly over the icy barrens of Frozen Strait to the west of Southampton Island, and arctic foxes scavenge for whatever sources of meat are to be found in the snow-covered tundra. Ptarmigans huddle in snow burrows or among rock crevices, spending the few daylight hours to seek out willow buds for sustenance and to watch the sky above for gyrfalcons and snowy owls. It is a world where the hunter, the hunted, and the hiding places are all white and in which only the hardiest of plants and animals survive. But it is also a world in which the end of every winter is an annual rebirth, an instant genesis during which almost every day sees the arrival of a new migrant bird, the blooming of a new flower, or the hatching of a new swarm of insects. The deathly stillness of the arctic night is replaced by the welcome sounds of breaking ice, of territorial ptarmigans, and of migrating waterfowl.

Now it is early June. Snow still lies thick on the mountains far to the north of the Bay of God's Mercy, but the sun rises higher in the sky, barely dipping each evening below Roes Welcome Sound beyond Cape Kendell. The pack ice is slowly breaking up, with leads of open water appearing here and there. Along the gravel ridges, inland from the high-tide line, bare ground and lichens appear as the snow melts under the warmth of the rising sun. A slight breeze is blowing out of the southwest, across a hundred miles of ice, from the coastal mainland

of Keewatin. Suddenly, below the scudding clouds, a string of birds appears, scattered across the sky like the beads of a broken necklace. Behind the first group come others, and more behind them. They are the first geese of the year. In family groups of five to twenty birds, they pass steadily northeastward toward the Bay of God's Mercy. Most of them are the white khanguks, but nearly a third are the blue khaviks. Farther to the east, other flocks are arriving from the southeast, headed for Bear Cove and East Bay. Within a few days, 25,000 snow geese will arrive at Boas River, 20,000 at East Bay, and 1,000 at Bear Cove.[1]

The adult geese are paired on arrival, the pair bonds having been gradually developed during individual associations of a year or more. Not surprisingly, most of the pairs consist of males and females of the white phase, and a majority of the blue-phase birds are similarly paired with like-colored ones. Yet, one sees many pairs made up of both color phases, usually a blue-phase male with a white female.

Two of the birds in the first flock to arrive at the Bay of God's Mercy are a three-year-old white-headed khavik, mated with a khanguk of the same age. Like most of the others in their age group, they have been mated for more than a year but have not previously bred. The female is now heavy with subcutaneous fat, and her ovaries are already enlarging. The pair quickly makes its way over the tundra flats, where tussocks of sedge and cotton grass are beginning to appear among the melting snow fields. These slight rises are the first to become completely snow free, and will be the driest nesting sites available on this soggy plain. Grassy islands at the mouth of the Boas River attract many of the geese; in such places they can nest in relative safety from arctic foxes.

After a nest site is chosen, a territory must be established, and the pair spends a few hectic days as the male evicts first one, then another intruder from the slight elevation that is to be the location of the female's nest. When she has finished a shallow nesting scrape, forming the bowl of her nest, she stretches out and begins to pluck the vegetation within her reach, heaping it into a low pile around the scrape. The nest bowl is surprisingly small, only eight inches across and four inches deep. Around this depression the khanguk constructs a low mound of weeds and shredded mosses two feet across and five inches high. Fine grasses form the nest lining and are later supplemented with a luxuriant layer of breast feathers and down.[2]

With the completion of her nest, the khanguk promptly deposits her first egg. Initially pure white, oval, and with a finely granulated sheen, it will gradually acquire a yellowish stain. Elsewhere in the colony the other females are also starting their clutches. The entire colony will complete its nest construction within ten days, and all of the eggs will be deposited within twelve days after the completion of the first nest. This amazing degree of colony synchronization reflects the critical importance of time in the short arctic summer; even a few days' delay beyond the optimum time for initiating breeding may doom the young, who might not be fully fledged before the first fall storms. Under the best of conditions the geese have no more than 105 days to complete their reproductive activities; with the unfavorable conditions caused by a late spring thaw and early return of winter, they may have as few as 83 days.[3]

Now, with the first egg in the nest, the khanguk begins to pluck body feathers and whitish down from her lower breast. Little will be used to cover the first egg, but as each day passes, the female adds more during her visits to the nest. Except when laying her eggs, she remains off the nest, which is closely guarded by her mate. Keeping a wary eye out for the ishoongok (jaegers), nawyavik (gulls), tooloogak (raven), and tiraganiok (arctic fox), the khanguk feeds ravenously, in preparation for the coming fast during incubation. She will lay five eggs, one during each of four successive days, followed by two days of rest, and a fifth egg on the seventh day. Some females, mainly those who begin laying very early, may lay as many as seven eggs, but those initiating their nests late may lay only three or four. During the egg-laying period the greatest egg losses result from stealing of individual eggs by jaegers while the nest is left unguarded. Arctic foxes sometimes also cause considerable egg losses during this period, but after incubation begins they are driven out of the territory by the adults. Egg losses to gulls are usually small, but the larger gulls are often serious gosling predators.[4]

It is now June 20. The nesting grounds have been free of snow for two weeks. The last egg has been laid, and many of the females have begun incubation. A few pairs have lost their entire clutches to the foxes or jaegers, and, since it is too late to begin a new clutch, these birds gradually leave the nesting colony to await their summer molt.

Scattered across the nesting grounds are a few large glacial boulders. Each supports a herring gull nest. These birds too keep a close watch for untended goose nests and waste little time in investigating any left untended for even a few minutes. At times gull and goose nests may be placed within a few yards of one another, but in such cases the goose is curiously immune to predation by the gull. Apparently the gull's predatory tendencies are inhibited within its own nesting territory; the presence of the gull thus confers upon the goose a degree of protection from other nest predators. Snow geese will also sometimes place their nests within the territories of snowy owls, gaining the benefits of protection from arctic foxes, for the owls will drive foxes away from their nesting areas.[5]

With the completion of her five-egg clutch, the khanguk begins her 23-day incubation period. During the first half of this period she will take short daily foraging breaks once a day, but during the latter part of incubation will rarely leave the nest. The male will remain nearby to help defend the nest, but, should the female have to leave it for any reason, he will not take over incubation. Much of the time he will remain quietly beside his nesting female, or stand a short distance away, constantly alert. The female likewise sits as low and inconspicuously as her white body will permit, her head resting comfortably on her back. The colony is strangely silent, a sharp contrast to the noise and confusion of the first few days of territorial establishment and nest building.

The snow geese are not the only nesting occupants of the low tundra. Besides the herring gulls are Sabine's gulls (akkigeriat-suk) and arctic terns (imakotailak). Several female oldsquaw ducks (uhgik) have their nests well concealed in the grass tundra beside the river, and the dead-grass color of these birds keeps them well hidden from aerial predators. Offshore, some of the boldly patterned male king eiders (kingalik) can still be seen, but these will soon migrate to their summer molting grounds along the west coast of Greenland, some thousand miles to the east.[6] Close to the tide line, a few nests of the brant goose (nugulungnuk) can be found, while occasional small Canada geese (nekilik) share the mid-river hummocks with the resident snow geese. Other birds nesting in or near the snow goose colony are the red-throated loons (kokshouk), red phalaropes (shiakuk), and various sandpipers. From a boulder-strewn hill-side in the distance come the barking calls of a cock willow ptarmigan (akigivik), and the melodic cries of a male oldsquaw duck occasionally drift in across the bay. Snowy owls (ookpik) and rough-legged hawks (kahyook) intermittently fly by the colony, and snow buntings (kopernoak) nest in rock or log crevices.[7]

The Eskimos know all these birds well, and their interest in them is not determined simply by whether or not they are large enough to provide a suitable meal. The birds are their friends and animal cousins, and even the lowliest of them might rep-resent a reincarnation of an ancestor, or of a human who has been miraculously transformed, as suggested by the following story:

KATSU, *an old woman, had an adopted son. One day while the boy was out in his kayak there arose a strong land-breeze. The boy tried hard to reach the shore, but in vain. For three days he struggled against the wind. The old woman, who saw him, ran up and down the beach, crying, "Grandson, paddle, paddle harder!" His face be-came quite red from the effort, and blood began to stream over his clothing. Still the old woman continued to shout to him, "Grandson, paddle, paddle, paddle harder! I have*

*no other boy. Paddle harder!" And then she burst into
tears, wailing, "Ah, ah, ah! Ah, ah, ah, kayalau!" She wore
long boots; and as she had been walking up and down the
beach a great deal, the soles began to turn up. The boy's
strength gave out, and he began to drift away. He became
transformed into a phalarope. The woman kept on walking
until the soles of her boots were all turned up, and her
clothing was covered with blood. She was transformed into
a loon.*[8]

In another story from the same area, a boy and his grandmother are similarly transformed:

*One evening a boy asked his grandmother to tell him a
story; but she only replied, "Go to bed and sleep. I have
no story to tell." Then the boy began to cry and insisted
that she should tell him a story. Then the old woman began
to rock herself from side to side and to say, "I will tell you
a story. I will tell you a long story about the lemming
without hair, that was in that place in the porch there. It
wanted to stay under my arm to keep warm. It had no hair,
and it cried, when it jumped up to its bed, 'Too, too,
too!' " The boy became frightened, and ran away. He was
transformed into a snow bunting. The old woman searched
for him everywhere, but could not find him, and finally she
gave up looking and sat down to cry. The tears ran down
her face, and she kept rubbing her eyes until they became
quite red and the skin came off. She had a small skin bag
which she put on her chest, close to her neck. She became
a ptarmigan.*

In still another story, a bear is transformed into geese:

*Arawi'kdjuaq and his wife lived in Saumia. Their son
was lost while hunting in his kayak, and the parents set out
to search for him. They followed the shore of the sea along
Saumia to the head of Cumberland Sound, down the west
side, and then up to Lake Netchillik. They crossed the lake
and camped on the bank of its outlet. One day a huge bear*

came up to their hut. It was as large as a good-sized island. When they saw it coming, they were much afraid. The woman said, "Oh, bear! this country is not fit for you to live in"; and, turning to her husband, she continued, "What kind of an animal fears man? We cannot get the better of that monster in its present shape. Let us transform it into geese!" Then she shouted, "Geese!" and immediately a cloud of geese arose from the bear's body.

Geese appear in the legends and stories of Eskimos in a variety of ways. In one story that is commonly told on both sides of Hudson Bay, an owl or hawk attempts to mate with geese. A version from the west side of Hudson Bay is as follows:

There was once an owl that took a wife from among the wild geese. But when the time came for the wild geese to fly away before the winter came, to other lands, the wild geese said:

"We shall come back again next year. You had better stay here in your own country and wait for us. You cannot paddle a kayak, and you would be drowned when you got tired. We have to fly across the great sea."

"I will go too," said the owl. "When they settle on the water to rest, I will keep hovering up above on outspread wings . . ."

The owl would not take the advice of the wild geese, and so when they flew away in the autumn, it flew with them. It flew a long, long way, but when the wild geese wanted to rest, they settled on the water, while the owl hovered in the air above. But one day the owl was so tired that it could keep up no longer, and the wild geese had to sit close together in the water so that it could rest on them. But they soon got tired of this. And one day, when the owl wanted to rest as usual, they suddenly swam apart, so that the owl fell into the water.

"The water is coming right up to my armpits!" cried the owl.

But the wild geese rose up and flew away.[9]

The legend of a mating between a man and a goose is also widespread among the Eskimos of Canada and Alaska. One of the versions has been provided by Diamond Jenness:

A man once found a gray goose bathing. He stole her clothes, and when she came out of the water and was looking for them he rushed out and seized her. Then he made her put on his own clothes so that she could not run away, and took her home to be his wife. In time they had a child. But the gray goose was not happy; her husband was always urging her to eat meat when what she craved for was grass. At last she determined to leave him and to take her child away with her; but when the mother rose on the wing the child was unable to follow; it merely fluttered along the ground. Its mother said, "Cry ni·l ni·l ni·l." As soon as the young bird repeated this cry it was able to rise into the air and they flew away together.[10]

From her nesting site in the goose colony, the khanguk cautiously lifts her head and surveys her world. Thirty feet away, her male stands silently in wait and occasionally pecks at the sedges and grasses around him. For a short period each day the khanguk will get off her nest and leave it long enough to obtain a quick meal, while her nest is closely guarded by her mate. Yet, her urge to incubate progressively overrides her hunger, and, as the incubation period proceeds, she spends less and less time away from the nest and increasingly begins to feel the signs of impending starvation. The Arctic is an intolerant host; if the eggs are to hatch, the female must be willing to sacrifice her energy reserves for their protection and incubation.

Before the creation, the world was a wide waste of water, without any inhabitants, except a few geese, which from some unknown parts paid occasional visits.

Weese-ke-jak found upon questioning them that they came from a country far away in the distant south, where there was plenty of land. Weese-ke-jak lost no time in making a bargain with the geese, that they would bring him a sample of earth on their next visit, which they did.

With the earth thus brought to him, Weese-ke-jak made the world, which he adorned with grass, trees, and herbs. This was followed by the creation of all the animals, reptiles, fowls, and fish.

—*Myth of the Bungees Cree*[11]

CHAPTER 3

Moon of Young Birds in the Nests

THREE WEEKS HAVE passed since Khanguk began her incubation period. A full five pounds at the onset of incubation, she now weighs less than four. Her breast muscles have so shriveled that her sharp-pointed keel almost protrudes from her skin; she is both weak and sensitive to the cold. Many of the other females in the colony, perhaps having had less fat reserves at the beginning of incubation, have been forced to leave their nests and forage to avoid starvation, thus abandoning their eggs to the ever-present gulls and jaegers. Others have succumbed to starvation or freezing, steadfastly sitting on their nests, dying quietly only a few days before their eggs were due to hatch. In some years a fifth of the colony's nests are thus doomed to failure in the late stages of incubation. The males fare only slightly better. Remaining near the nest to protect it, they too have had little time for foraging, and their average weight is often reduced to an emaciated four pounds.[1]

Now, just three weeks from the time Khanguk began incubation, her clutch begins to pip. A slight metallic tapping sound comes from the eggs; a series of cracks appears near their larger ends. Soon the cracks enlarge and progressively spread around the larger end of the egg, as deftly and surely as if a chisel were being operated from the inner surface. The gosling is repeatedly jerking its bill upward by means of reflexive muscle action, each jerk causing the egg tooth to crack the shell a little more, and between jerks shifts the axis of its body slightly within the shell, so that each pipping movement will be slightly displaced from the last. The four first-laid eggs will complete their hatching almost simultaneously, just over 23 days after incubation was begun. The last-laid egg will not hatch for another day and, as is common with the last eggs of large clutches, this gosling will be weaker than those produced from the earlier eggs.[2]

In the case of Khanguk's clutch, the first four goslings to hatch include two males and two females. The males and one of the females are all a dark, greenish gray, with a pale lemon mark on the throat, and with black bills, feet, and legs. The remaining female, as well as the last-hatched gosling, a male, are mostly lemon yellow, especially on the sides of the head and throat, shading to dusky on the back. Their feet and legs are a dusky green, with a hint of pale violet on the insides of the legs and the webs of the feet. These lemon-colored downies are of the type that will produce white-phase adults, while the duskier ones will mature into blue-phase adults.

Now the nest cup is filled with squirming youngsters, which huddle under their mother's breast feathers and occasionally peep out over the side of the nest. The nest is crowded with young and littered with empty egg shells, so the newly hatched goslings must struggle to avoid being trampled or smothered to death.

By the next morning, the family is ready to leave the nest. The goslings are now fully rested from their exertions in escaping the confines of egg shells, and the undigested portions of their yolk sacs can see them through several days without eating. Yet, they are thirsty, and the mother has a strong urge to leave the nesting area to find a place where she can feed and begin to replenish her energy reserves.

So they leave their nest for good. Four of the goslings follow closely behind their parents, running nimbly about, swimming through shallow pools, and pecking at insects. But the last-hatched lemon-colored youngster falls farther and farther behind, in spite of the calls of its parents. There is a swoop, a quick jab, and the gosling is suddenly lifeless, to be carried away and eaten at a herring gull's leisure.

In early July the daylight period lasts for 24 hours. The sun's warmth has produced abundant insect life, especially mosquitoes. These are relished by the goslings, whose appetites are boundless, and they grow astonishingly fast. Most of the colony's successfully hatched broods have now left their nests; the younger broods consisting of four or five goslings; the older ones, three or four surviving young.

Even before the hatching of the last clutch, some of the older snow geese had become flightless as a result of their postnuptial molt. These were the immature non-breeders who had remained largely to themselves at the edges of the breeding colony. Unsuccessful breeders later joined this group, and they lost more and more of their feathers until the loss of their primary and secondary flight feathers rendered them completely flightless for about 24 days.[3]

The flightless period is a particularly dangerous time for waterfowl. Not only are they especially vulnerable to large predators, but also the energy demands imposed on the birds by the growth of a completely new generation of feathers is substantial. The breast muscles may wither even more than they did during incubation, but the gizzard, which had been quite small then, increases to more than twice its former size and the leg muscles also enlarge.[4]

The vulnerability of flightless geese to capture was well known and widely practiced by the natives of arctic North America as well as Iceland. Graham Cooch has described the procedure:

The Eskimo technique is simple but effective. A trapping drive is initiated by a group of men walking on a course nearly parallel to that of a large flock of geese. The birds see figures loom up through the heat haze, but, unless it becomes immediately apparent that these figures are coming directly toward them, they merely walk slowly away from the disturbance. If approached directly, many escape. The technique is to approach them indirectly, leaving a man behind from time to time to check their retreat in his direction. The drivers, still walking, try to keep the birds slowly circling in one general direction, otherwise they take fright and scatter. The process is continued until one man is left walking. It is often necessary for one driver to run quickly ahead of the flock to complete the circle. The drivers left behind from time to time remain hidden until it becomes apparent that one member has "headed" the flock and that the geese are now starting to run back toward their original feeding area. No matter which way the geese turn, their progress is blocked by figures suddenly looming up on the horizon. Finally the geese become completely muddled and give up. They stand in a vast milling mob, chattering so loudly that vocal communication among the drivers is difficult.

The birds are now under control. All the drivers begin to close in on the flock, except one who acts as a "Judas Goat." He walks off in the direction of the corral, never looking back. The birds move away from the encircling drivers and follow the one who is apparently retreating.

When the man leading the flock reaches the corral he walks through the entrance and climbs out at the end. The geese crowd into the pen.[5]

A Chippewa legend, as recounted by William Jones, suggests that this tribe of Indians also knew something of capturing flightless geese:

While Nänabushu was traveling about, he soon came out upon a brook; he followed its course till at last it (opened out into) a large river. Then presently he came in sight of a lake; very beautiful was the place where the river flowed out (into the lake). While Nänabushu was looking about, (he saw) an island of sand; he saw some Goslings, very numerous were they. Nänabushu, simpleton that he was, went running out toward the land, he went to get some balsam-boughs; in his old soiled blanket he wrapped them. He made a pack of the balsams, a very heavy pack did the balsams make. And so when he started on his way, he had his hands on the tump-line (running from the forehead back over the shoulders). When he came into view (round *a point of land), up spoke a big Goose: "Nänabushu is coming into view (round the point). Do you (not) flee, for something shall we be told."*

But the Goslings did not fly away. Lo, they were addressed by Nänabushu saying: "Truly am I sad at heart whenever I fail to see my little brothers. Now, truly a merry time is going at the place from whence I come; for at that place are the people dancing together. Wonderfully good are the songs that they sing. Pray, let me make you dance. Now, these that I have on my back are those very songs. And down at this spot will I lay the songs. I will fix a place yonder where I will devote (myself) to making you dance. Handsome will be the dance-lodge that I will make." Nänabushu thereupon set to work making it, with balsams he made a stockade; at only such a height that it could not be taken at a leap was how high he made his dance-lodge. "It is now time for us to begin dancing together. Hither, now come you out of the water."

To be sure, the Goslings came out of the water.

"Harken! I will tell you how you are to act. According as I sing, so do you when you dance. Do you take pains. Don't you fail in anything. Now is the time for you to enter into the dance-lodge."

Then in went the Goslings, likewise the Loon; and also the Diver entered in.[6]

For the geese that succeed in hatching a brood of goslings, the timing of the postnuptial molt must be remarkably precise. Within six weeks after hatching, the brood will be ready to embark on its first flights, and during the same interval the adults must complete their own molts in order to be ready to leave the breeding grounds for the long trip south. Should the adults begin their molts too early, they will be unable to protect adequately their brood at its most vulnerable period, and may not themselves survive the additional energy demands of molting so soon after the stress of incubation. Yet a delay of the molt until the young are about to fledge may mean that the adults are still flightless when the first storms of fall descend on the breeding grounds.

Natural selection has provided the geese with a compromise solution. The adults become flightless about twenty days after their broods have hatched. By then the chicks are not defenseless, and the adults have also begun to recover from their condition of near starvation. Frequently, one of the members of the pair becomes flightless several days in advance of the other, thus reducing the time during which both parents are simultaneously flightless. In most cases, the adults will have regained their powers of flight a few days in advance of the six-week fledging period of the brood. Before the adults begin their wing molt, they lead their young from the nesting grounds and, with hundreds of other geese, move to large lakes several miles inland, where they will be well protected from terrestrial predators during the flightless period.

Thus Khavik, Khanguk, and their brood of four well-grown youngsters are approaching the time that they will all be able to fly. The young geese are still clumsy and gawky-looking, with traces of down still clinging to the tips of the feathers that are now emerging from their lower back and rump regions. The heads and necks of the three young blue-phase geese are almost uniformly slate gray, grading to darker gray on their backs, and with paler bellies. The newly emerging flight feathers are a much duller brownish slate color. A brownish hue outlines the lesser wing coverts on the upper forewings. The greater wing coverts directly before the flight feathers, the lower back, and the upper-tail coverts are a pale gray. The tail feathers are slate gray, with silvery edges. The only suggestion of the white-headed condition of the adults is a white chin patch which sometimes extends to the base of the upper mandible. The bill and feet are still nearly black, but a suffusion of pink will increase as the birds grow older.

The young khavik more closely resembles her mother, but is distinctly grayish, especially on her upperparts. Brownish gray mottles her head and neck, especially on the crown; her back and upper wing coverts are ashy gray with lighter edges. Her primaries are slate-colored, while the white-edged secondaries are distinctly lighter. The whitest part of the young khavik's plumage is her tail and its coverts. The violet tints on her legs and feet will become more evident as she grows older, and shades of purple, rose, and orange will gradually supplant the black of her bill.

By the beginning of September the goslings are approaching two months of age. Their body weights have multiplied twenty-fold since hatching, from two and one-half to more than fifty ounces. A hint of winter chills the air, the grass has already turned brown. Now the geese are becoming increasingly restless. For no apparent reason, flocks suddenly leap into the air, fly about, and land again, calling loudly. They feed desultorily on the last remaining bits of green grass and sedges that are to be found. Unfledged loons still swim about in the shallow lakes, and snowy owls still feed their young. Yet, flocks of whistling swans (kugjuk) are already gathering for their fall flight across Hudson Bay, and the oldsquaws and eiders have already departed with their fledged broods. The short arctic summer is over; it is time to leave.

One day a man whose mind was open to the teaching of the powers wandered on the prairie. As he walked, his eyes upon the ground, he spied a bird's nest hidden in the grass, and arrested his feet just in time to prevent stepping on it. He paused to look at the little nest tucked away so snug and warm, and noted that it held six eggs and that a peeping sound came from some of them. While he watched, one moved and soon a tiny bill pushed through the shell, uttering a shrill cry. At once the parent birds answered and he looked up to see where they were. They were not far off; they were flying about in search of food, chirping the while to each other and now and then calling to the little one in the nest.

The homely scene stirred the heart and the thoughts of the man as he stood there under the clear sky, glancing upward toward the old birds and then down to the helpless young in the nest at his feet. As he looked he thought of his people, who were so often careless and thoughtless of their children's needs, and his mind brooded over the matter. After many days he desired to see the nest again. So he went to the place where he had found it, and there it was as safe as when he left it. But a change had taken place. It was now full to overflowing with little birds, who were stretching their wings, balancing on their little legs and making ready to fly, while the parents with encouraging calls were coaxing the fledglings to venture forth.

"Ah!" said the man, "if my people would only learn of the birds, and, like them, care for their young and provide for their future, homes would be full and happy, and our tribe be strong and prosperous."

—Song of the Bird's Nest, Hako Ceremony[7]

CHAPTER 4

South to the Spirit Waters

JAMES BAY PROJECTS southward from the base of Hudson Bay like the tail of a giant beaver. From Southampton Island's Cape Low to the entrance of James Bay at Cape Henrietta Maria it is a minimum above-water flight of nearly 600 miles. The same is true of the distance from Eskimo Point on the Keewatin mainland to the Cape. From the Foxe Peninsula of Baffin Island, the departure point for the large goose population breeding at Bowman Bay, the minimum air distance to James Bay is closer to 700 miles. Such a non-stop flight might well tax the strength of the newly fledged goslings. Alternatively, the shorelines of Hudson Bay might be followed, providing a number of convenient resting and foraging places without seriously increasing the total length of the journey. This, in fact, is the way that the trip is actually made.

J. Dewey Soper believed that the snow geese from Southampton Island must fly southeasterly across Evans Strait to Cape Wolstenholm on the Ungava Peninsula before heading south. Dr. George Sutton's observation of the geese leaving Cape Low in a southeasterly direction toward Coates Island supported this conclusion. A comparable distance separates Cape Wolstenholm from the southern tip of Baffin Island's Foxe Peninsula, and it was evident to Soper that the Baffin Island goose population must cross this part of the Hudson Strait before proceeding southward along the east coast of Hudson Bay toward James Bay.

On the basis of more recent observations, and especially from the information provided by banding studies, it is now evident that the fall migration pathways from Southampton and Baffin islands do not merge on the eastern shore of Hudson Bay as Soper believed, but rather remain relatively separate from one another.

After passing Cape Wolstenholm, the geese from Baffin Island gradually work their way southward, hugging the coast and leisurely foraging in the shallow marshes and tidal flats along the east coast of Hudson Bay. By the middle of September they have reached Cape Jones at the northeastern end of James Bay and will soon find a perfect place to rest and feed in the coastal marshes and tidal flats of that shallow bay.[1]

A quite different situation is typical of the birds from Boas River. Our family of snow geese, the two adults and the four surviving goslings, have taken a southwesterly course upon leaving Southampton Island, and after a flight of little more than a hundred miles gain sight of the mainland just south of Chesterfield Inlet. It is about two hundred additional miles to Eskimo Point, where the adults and progeny of a 15,000-bird snow goose colony are also preparing to leave their nesting grounds. The arrival of the Southampton Island birds more than trebles their number, and a flock of some 50,000 birds is now gradually working its way down the west coast of Hudson Bay.

Another 150 miles to the south is Cape Churchill, and a few miles to the west lies La Pérouse Bay. In the early 1950s snow geese began nesting in small numbers there, and by the late 1960s nearly 2,000 birds were in the colony. Now, just before mid-September, these birds join the great flocks from farther north and with them begin moving southeasterly along the coast.[2]

One last contingent of snow geese will join the flocks before they rendezvous with those from Baffin Island. These are the birds that now nest at Cape Henrietta Maria, the world's southernmost known snow goose nesting colony. It began apparently in the late 1940s but was not discovered by ornithologists for another decade. By 1970 it contained about 40,000 birds.[3]

As the geese leave Cape Churchill, their flightlines move increasingly from the most direct route between Hudson Bay and the marshes of the eastern Dakotas. Some begin to pull away from the main flocks moving southeasterly and instead follow the courses of the Nelson, Severn, and Winisk rivers in a south-westerly direction. This route will take them across the lake-studded and conifer-dominated forests of western Ontario, between Lake Winnipeg and Lake Superior, and finally out over the prairies of central Minnesota and the eastern Dakotas.

The great flocks have now sorted out into three segments. One group, from breeding grounds in Southampton Island and the west coast of Hudson Bay, heads in a southwesterly direction toward the eastern Dakotas, where it will soon find both refuge and tragedy at Sand Lake. A small part of this flock will continue down along the coast of Hudson Bay to southern James Bay. Here, in mid-September, they will meet and mix with a third group, the hundreds of thousands of blue-phase birds that have just arrived from Baffin Island. Perhaps 95 per cent of this goose congregation will be lesser snow geese, nearly all of the blue phase, while most of the remainder will be Canada geese. Well offshore, especially around some of the islands, a few brant are to be found. For a few weeks between mid-September and late October, James Bay will be one of the world's greatest convocations of geese, but dominated by the wavies.

A dozen or more small rivers empty into the southern end of James Bay, which because of its shallowness at the southern tip forms wide expanses of tidal flats between the bay proper and the shoreline. On these muddy flats, and in the mouths of the rivers emptying into the bay, the geese congregate. In the broad belt between the minimum tide line and the maximum high-tide mark, there are several plant zones. The zone closest to the shoreline is dominated by plants that can tolerate periodic flooding by salt water, including two species of bulrushes, a species of spike rush, and other salt-tolerant herbs. Behind this zone is one that is flooded infrequently, and its typical plants include horsetails, a variety of sedges, bulrushes, spike rushes, and a number of broad-leaved herbaceous plants. Behind this zone is one dominated by several species of willows, with various herbs and grasses growing below. This last zone is transitional with

the true coniferous forest, or taiga, whose tipi-like trees rise behind the bay and continue in an almost uninterrupted manner to the Great Lakes, over 300 miles to the south.[4]

The geese feed on abundant food, particularly the horsetails, bulrushes, and sedges, all of which grow sufficiently near the shoreline to render the birds fairly safe from predators and hunters. However, the geese also often fly into the adjacent scrub forest to feed on the ripening berry crop, where they may be hunted much more easily. For the Cree Indians, who have hunted the geese of James Bay for uncounted generations, it was necessary to obtain materials for blinds in the willow zone and carry them out into the shoreline zone, sometimes as far as two or three miles.

The earliest description of their manner of goose-hunting was provided by J. R. Forster in 1772:

> *The Indians have a peculiar method of killing all these species of geese, and likewise swans. As these birds fly regularly along the marsh, the Indians range themselves in a line across the marsh, from the wood to high-water mark, about musket shot from each other, so as to be sure of intercepting any geese which fly that way. Each person conceals himself, by putting round him some brushwood; they likewise make artificial geese of sticks and mud, placing them at a short distance from themselves, in order to decoy the real geese within shot; thus prepared they sit down, and keep a good lookout; and as soon as the flock appears they all lie down, imitating the call or note of geese, which these birds no sooner hear, and perceive the decoys, than they go straight down toward them; then the Indians rise on their knees, and discharge one, two, or three guns each, killing two or even three geese at each shot, for they are very expert.[5]*

By the time the geese have reached James Bay, they have more than recovered the weight they lost during the long breeding season. Adult males now average more than six pounds, while juvenile males weigh only about a pound less. Adult females average nearly five and a half pounds, and juveniles nearly five. Both the adults and juveniles will gain a few additional ounces during the approximate month they spend on the James Bay flats.

During the period that the geese remain in James Bay in great numbers, the Indians shoot enough of them to last through the long winter. In the early 1950s, it was estimated that each of the approximately 800 native hunters might kill 100 birds per season, representing a total kill of some 75,000 birds. Nearly 5,000 Indians then lived in the James Bay district and, although this goose harvest might seem substantial, it was vital for the Indians' winter survival.

By late October, the geese that are still present in James Bay have become well endowed with a substantial layer of body fat, while their food supplies such as berries, sedges, and bulrush roots have become progressively scarcer. Further, a cold wind blows out of the northwest, and thin layers of ice rim the shoreline each morning. Then comes a clear day and a 20-mile-per-hour wind out of the northwest. By late afternoon one flock after another takes flight, and all set courses southward along the Kesagami River. Calling continuously, one flock begins where the next leaves off, and as the last rays of sunlight strike the spruces lining the eastern edge of James Bay, the sky is alive with migrating geese. Higher and higher they rise, so that, by the time they cross North Bay in southern Ontario, they are flying at between six and eight thousand feet, well out of the hearing and visual range of persons below. They fly all night, all of the next day, and by the morning of the third day the first fall migrants of the year drop into their winter quarters at Chenier au Tigre, Vermilion Parish, Louisiana. They have completed a non-stop 1,700-mile flight in less than 60 hours. This is not much longer than a theoretical minimum flight time of 42 hours on the basis of an average ground speed of 40 miles per hour.[6]

Seven hundred miles to the west of James Bay, Khanguk, Khavik, and their young are part of a large flock of geese crossing the Red River just north of Grand Forks, North Dakota.

Below are table-flat clay bottomlands, the ancient floor of Lake Agassiz, now planted nearly to the roadsides with sugar beets, flax, and spring wheat. Fifteen miles farther west, the geese fly over the sandy soils that mark an old river delta, now the home of some of the last surviving prairie chickens in North Dakota. Finally, the geese reach the gently rolling glacial drift plains of eastern North Dakota. Strewn among these˙ beautiful prairie-covered hills, like blue feathers drifting on a sea of grass, are a myriad of potholes, marshes, and shallow lakes. These wetlands were formed either by the random irregularities of the ground moraine, where waters gradually accumulated, or by melting masses of outwash glacial ice, leaving depressions of various sizes and shapes that filled with water. From the eastern Dakotas through southern Manitoba, the surface topography is studded with these small wetlands. Each is a self-sufficient eco-system, gaining enough water each winter through snow accumulation to see it through most or all of the short summer, and providing haven for a host of resident waterfowl, shore-birds, and land animals.[7]

Now the snow geese cautiously circle a large, shallow lake. They have already met hunters' gunfire on their flight across western Ontario and northern Minnesota. Seeing a flock of several hundred of their kind on the water below, they circle ever closer to the water. Finally, throwing caution to the winds, they sideslip downward amid a chorus of greeting calls from the geese below. They have arrived safely at Devils Lake, the lake once known as Minnewaukon (spirit waters) to the Dakotas.

Now, once again was Nänabushu traveling along, when he then saw some more geese that were in a lake. Thereupon he spoke to them, saying: "Pray, do you make me look the same as you." A long while was he coaxing them. At last, "All right," he was told. Accordingly by each one was he given a feather. And when the number of feathers was enough (to cover him), then truly like a goose was the look of Nänabushu. Up he also flew when he went about in company with the geese. And when it was getting well on towards the fall, "Therefore now is it time for us to be going away," he was told. Thereupon then up they rose on the wing, as on their way southward they went, (and) they sang:

"By way of the mountain-ranges do I fly along through the sky,

By way of the mountain-ranges do I fly along through the sky,

By way of the mountain-ranges do I fly along through the sky."

And then he was told: "Do not look everywhere, but straight toward the way we are bound do you look. For not far away do some people dwell in a town who shall be in the way of our course. Do not for any reason look. Everywhere will be heard the voices of the people shouting. Do not look at them."

When they came to where the people lived in a town, already were the geese seen flying past. "Hey! Just look at the geese! Truly big is one of the geese!" All sorts of noise did the people make. At last did Nänabushu look, whereupon he was accidentally hit on the wing, broken was his wing; and then down fell Nänabushu.

—Ojibwa legend[8]

CHAPTER 5

The Massacre of Sand Lake

In the Beginning, the Old Man and the Old Woman debated about whether people should die. The Old Man said, "People will never die." The Old Woman replied, "Oh, that will never do, because, if people live always, there will be too many people in the world." The Old Man answered, "Well, we do not want to die forever. We shall die for four days and then come to life again." "Oh, no," said the Old Woman, "it will be better to die forever, so that we shall be sorry for each other. We must have death in order that we may pity one another."

—Blackfoot myth[1]

SOMEWHERE, IN WHAT is now eastern North Dakota, a nameless river was born. Its birthplace was probably halfway between the present locations of Devils Lake and the Missouri River, in a shallow basin covered with the bluestem prairies that once nearly blanketed the eastern half of the state. Its time of birth is impossible to gauge. Like many wild things it was born an eon ago, it is born today and, fate willing, it will be born an eon hence. No records of such trivialities as the birth of a stream are kept by nature; the face of the earth records only those events and processes substantive enough to ieave a lasting image on its surface. Unpredictable spring thunderstorms periodically nourished the infant stream, but equally often it was seared by the summer sun, or it offered up its meager water to the thirsty bison that sometimes waded in it to drink or to cool themselves in its deeper pools.

As the river slowly grew, low shrubs and small trees such as willows replaced the tall prairie grasses that had initially sustained its life and had shaded it. Song sparrows and yellow warblers, which perched among the shrubs and built nests in their midst, supplanted the meadowlarks that had nested in the matted grasses near its edges. The vagaries of the glacier-shaped topography were such that the stream almost aimlessly wandered northeastward, not so much cutting a valley as conforming to the natural undulations of the prairie's mantle of glacial till. Here and there the stream overflowed its modest banks, especially in the early spring when snow meltwaters filled the stream bed and thus replenished the adjacent low meadows. Shore birds such as phalaropes, sandpipers, and yellowlegs, and waterfowl such as ducks, coots, and grebes found these shallow pools teeming with life. Each spring, rafts of ducks littered these ponds and phalanxes of wading birds lined their edges. Occasionally these birds visited the stream too, but more often it provided relative seclusion for mating birds avoiding the heavy traffic of the adjacent ponds.

The stream wandered onward, now cutting into a far bank in a graceful bend, now depositing its newly acquired wealth of silt on another bank farther downstream. Sometimes in this endless process of give and take, a bone or entire skeleton of a bison would be exposed, only to be later hidden again under a new deposit of silt. In this manner, the pages of the earth's history gradually turned, were rewritten, and replaced, perhaps with the newly added punctuation marks of a deer's remains, or the carcass of an unlucky rodent that drowned in the spring floods.

Then, some fifty miles east of its inconspicuous origins, the river turned decisively southward into a drainage system that was to bring it into confluence first with the Missouri, then the

Mississippi, and to eventually reach the Gulf of Mexico. Only a hundred miles farther east, another river, the Red, was just as persistently flowing northward, its waters ultimately to reach Hudson Bay. By this time, our river had gained sufficient respectability to be given a name, the James. To reach their ancestral wintering grounds on the Gulf Coast, the snow geese resting at Devils Lake need only follow the course of the James River.[2]

From the point where the James River turns southward to the general vicinity of Redfield, South Dakota, it cuts across the eastern Dakotas in a graceful eastward-directed arc resembling a gigantic hunting bow. An imaginary arrow, formed by the political boundary separating the two Dakotas, bisects its length. Just below the point where the arrow crosses the bow, the James River spreads out to form a broadened handgrip, which is Sand Lake. The name is misleading; it is actually a shallow reservoir formed by two low dams that back the river up into the adjacent prairies. Covering some 11,200 acres, Sand Lake was declared a national wildlife refuge in 1935. Yet, not until the mid-1940s did the snow geese incorporate the lake into their fall migratory tradition. Only a few hundred stopped there in 1944, but within five years the numbers had reached 10,000. By the late 1960s more than 100,000 snow geese annually poured into the small lake, which had then become ringed with hunting pits on the privately owned lands surrounding the refuge. The stage had been set for a bloody yearly slaughter.

In the fall of 1969 the hunters in the area about Sand Lake killed and retrieved an estimated 36,000 geese, and according to Glen Sherwood perhaps as many as 20,000 more were crippled and never retrieved. Others received less serious wounds that may have resulted in later mortality. This carnival of death attracted sportsmen from great distances. Lined up only a few feet from one another along refuge boundary fences, or hidden in pits in adjacent cornfields, many hunters knew little of what they were shooting at, and cared even less for how many birds they crippled. For many, at least, the geese were simply good targets, providing more exciting "sport" than shooting at inanimate targets, or an excuse to spend a drinking and hunting weekend with friends.[3]

Now, as the chill north winds of late October stream across the gently rolling uplands of the Coteau des Prairies, separating the drainages of the Missouri and upper Mississippi rivers, Khavik, Khanguk, and their young follow the James River southward toward Sand Lake. Ahead, tens of thousands of geese rest on the water, and circling birds overhead fill the sky above the refuge. Like a band of Indians attacking a wagon train, they circle ever closer and lower, constantly calling wildly, only to rise again as one after another of the birds in their midst suddenly tumbles from the sky in a death plunge.

Cautiously, Khavik leads his family downwind toward the lake, only very gradually losing altitude. A long, shallow approach, a sharp turn into the eye of the wind, and they will be able to sideslip almost vertically onto the water. They are now within a half mile of the lake, skimming sixty yards above the golden fields of prairie grasses and harvested corn. Abruptly, from a camouflaged pit directly below, a man appears, pointing the long barrel of a 12-gauge magnum directly at them. Khavik shrieks a warning, quickly veering and clawing for altitude. His white mate just beside him does likewise, but the slower reflexes of the goslings fail them. Three quick shots erupt from the automatic. The trailing blue gosling's right wing collapses, and he drops head-over-tail toward earth. The white female flying beside her stricken brother simultaneously feels the dull thud of buckshot in her abdomen. Streaming blood from belly to tail, she instinctively sets her wings and heads for the nearest water. As she falls away from her parents, she vainly struggles to regain altitude as the ground rises to meet her. But it is too late. As her strength fades and her senses dim, she crashes headlong into a cottonwood tree. Bouncing off a large branch that nearly rips one wing from its socket, she is thrown upside down into a thick clump of snowberry bushes.

Khavik, his mate, and the surviving blue goslings are now well out of shotgun range and within the refuge boundaries. Yet, hoping that a stray pellet might strike a vital organ, the hunters continue to shoot in their general direction. As Khanguk leads her two goslings to the safety of water, Khavik turns back, calling frantically for his two missing offspring. Circling over the pit well out of shotgun range, he sees a hunter chasing the blue gosling with the broken wing. Catching him at last, the hunter quickly wrings his neck and, holding him by one leg, carries the bird back toward the pit, his head bumping along the ground. For him, at least, death has come swiftly. The hunter calls to a companion in the nearby pit, "I caught the blue cripple, but the white one went down beyond the retrieval zone." "Never mind," the other replies, "we can't waste a lot of time running around after cripples; there will be lots more coming before the day is over." Nodding in unspoken agreement, the man climbs back into his pit and lights another cigarette. Mindlessly, he stuffs the stub of the one he just finished between the dead blue gosling's mandibles, which had just begun to acquire the beautiful reddish tints characteristic of fully grown birds.

Khavik circles back downwind toward where he saw his white daughter disappear. Calling constantly, he scans the ground below for a sign of life. Hidden by the branches of the snowberry bush, the young female dimly hears his calls. By now, her lungs have filled with blood, and as she opens her bill her only reply is a gurgling sound. Lying helplessly on her back, feet still uselessly paddling the air, she cannot see that the bloody wound on her abdomen has stained her entire underparts with red. Drawing on her last remaining strength, she raises her head and through dimming eyes gains a final glimpse of her white-headed father passing above. Then her feet slowly cease their paddling, her body gives a final convulsive quiver, and she is dead. Overhead, white feathers torn from her body by the fusillade of gunfire still drift in the wind, eventually settling and floating as lightly as phalaropes on the surface of the lake.

For Khavik, there is nothing left to do but to find the rest of his family among the thousands of geese milling about on the lake's surface. Time after time he flies the length of the lake, calling constantly. Finally, he recognizes the familiar notes of his mate in the pandemonium of goose sounds that envelop him. Exhausted, he drops into the water beside her. The two remaining goslings, a male and a female, are untouched by gunfire. His mate has suffered only a minor wound, where a single buckshot pellet has entered her breast and lodged near the keel. Had she been fifteen yards lower, it would probably have passed through the thin keel and entered her heart cavity. As it is, she will be temporarily slowed, but should eventually heal.*

Two hundred yards from the edge of the lake, the warmth of the white gosling's body slowly escapes, and her limbs stiffen in the cold. Soon, the energy she had stored up in her body on an arctic island 1,200 miles to the north will become part of the protoplasm of a South Dakota red fox. Her bones will be scattered and left to bleach on the prairie, eventually becoming covered with fallen cottonwood leaves and the snows of winter. The following spring will see a pasque flower blooming above her buried keel, the plant's roots enveloping it and extracting from it the last remaining nutrients. In this fashion an arctic tundra ecosystem gives sustenance to a Dakota prairie, and thus does life reflect the mirror image of death.

> *"When I look back now from this high hill of my old age, I can still see the butchered women and children lying heaped and scattered all along the gulch as plain as when I saw them with eyes still young. And I can see that something else died there in the bloody mud, and was buried in the blizzard. A people's dream died there. It was a beautiful dream."*
>
> —Black Elk (1863–1950)[4]

---

* It has been estimated on the basis of banding recoveries from lesser snow geese banded in the Pacific Flyway that there is a mortality rate of about 49 per cent for immature birds during the twelve months following banding. Of this total immature mortality, nearly 70 per cent results from hunting activity. The annual mortality rate of birds banded as adults is only half that of immatures, but again over 60 per cent of this mortality was estimated to be a result of hunting.

CHAPTER 6

Moon of the Falling Leaves

Then the bay horse wheeled to where the great white giant lives (the north) and said: "Behold!" And yonder there were twelve white horses all abreast. Their manes were flowing like a blizzard wind and from their noses came a roaring, and all about them white geese soared and circled.

—The great vision of Black Elk[1]

THE GREAT BEAR now prowls high in the northern sky, and the swan flies down the spirit path toward the campfires of the setting sun. An icy breath pours forth from the land of the great white giant, and the winds have stripped the rustling trees of the last of their arrowhead leaves. The Indiangrass and bluestem have turned the color of pipestone, and a coyote wails at the frosty moon. It is early in November, the Moon of the Falling Leaves.

Two weeks have passed since Khavik and his family arrived at Sand Lake. Most of the snow geese have already moved on southward, but Khanguk's breast wound had prevented an early departure for the family. Now, with the first blizzard of winter sweeping downward out of North Dakota, they must be on their way.

Overcast skies prevent night navigation, so the family leaves early one morning, a strong north wind at their backs. Striking out in a southerly direction, the geese will initially follow the valley of the James River. Eventually they will reach the point

where the James flows into the much larger Missouri River in the vicinity of Yankton, South Dakota.

Over a century and a half earlier, Lewis and Clark had passed the mouth of the James River during the fall of 1804 and again in 1806. In that general area they saw wild turkeys, passenger pigeons, prairie chickens, and sharp-tailed grouse, and the land was a virgin wilderness. Farther upstream, near the mouth of the Little Missouri, they also observed whooping cranes, as well as both "white brant" and "gray brant," and they wondered whether the two brant types might be the same or two different species. Here, too, the painter George Catlin had come in the steamer *Yellow Stone* on its maiden trip up the Missouri in the early 1830s. At the mouth of the Niobrara River, only a few miles upstream from the mouth of the James, he listened as a Ponca chieftain told him of the slaughter of the bison that was already underway, and how his tribe would soon be extinct. Not only would the Indians soon be killed or driven from their lands, but the passenger pigeon was also destined to be exterminated, and the prairie chicken and whooping crane nearly so.[2]

By the time they reach the confluence of the James and Missouri rivers, the snow geese had already flown nearly 250 miles since leaving Sand Lake. Yet, a strong trailing wind helped them to complete this leg of the journey in less than five hours. Now they turn more easterly, following the deeper and wider valley of the Missouri on its gracefully curving sweep across northeastern Nebraska. Soon they are flying past the barren reservations of the poverty-stricken Winnebago and Omaha Indians. The Winnebagos surviving there are the progeny of a people evicted long before from their ancestral forested homelands in eastern Wisconsin. The Omahas on the reservation are captives in their own land, remnants of a once-proud tribe that lived along the banks of the Missouri. They, and the peaceful Pawnees, were virtually eliminated by smallpox only shortly after George Catlin studied and painted them.

A hundred miles downstream from its confluence with the James River, the Missouri makes one of several broad, horseshoelike bends that provide wide sandbars and potential resting sites for the geese. It is at one of these, DeSoto Bend, that the flock finds its first safe resting place since leaving Sand Lake, 350 miles to the north.

DeSoto National Wildlife Refuge now surrounds the old DeSoto Bend of the Missouri River, which was permanently isolated from the main stream bed of the Missouri River by the dredging in 1959 of a nearly straight channel across the tips of the oxbow. Thus, a lake shaped like a horseshoe was formed, and a tiny bit of Nebraska was consequently isolated on the Iowa side of the river. Surrounding the 700-acre lake are another 7,000 acres of refuge land, about half of which are now planted with corn, milo, winter wheat, and other crops on a share-cropping basis. The refuge's share is left standing for use by wildlife, although the snow geese feed on waste grain and winter wheat. Practically no geese stopped at DeSoto Bend before it was made a refuge in 1959 but, like Sand Lake, its usage by geese skyrocketed. The goose numbers increased annually each fall until they reached peak populations of up to 300,000 birds during the late 1960s and early 1970s. As many as a half million mallards also congregate there during fall, as well as small numbers of other dabbling ducks, Canada geese, and a sprinkling of diving ducks, mostly goldeneyes and mergansers.[3]

Now the snow goose flock circles the refuge cautiously. In the late afternoon sun, the hills on the Nebraska side of the river valley five miles away are tinted with violet in the shaded ravines, where the bur oaks still cling tightly to their rust-colored leaves. Along the river itself, cottonwoods and willows stand gaunt. Already stripped of their leaves, their buckskin-colored branches contrast with the rich blood-red tints of the red osier dogwoods below them. Following the wind to the southern end of the lake, the birds swing gracefully around the curve of the oxbow, and spiral downward to land at the northern end, where a heavy growth of cottonwoods and willows helps to cut the wind. The lake is already jam-packed with geese, while mallards mill among them and at the edges of the goose flock. Watching every move of the incoming geese are a pair of bald eagles, the first of the season to arrive on the refuge. Periodically, to be certain they have not overlooked any cripples, the eagles make a low pass over the swimming geese. Their curiosity satisfied, they return to a nearby cottonwood and continue their vigil.

Not far from the concentration of geese lies the wrecked hull of the steamship *Bertrand* which, when loaded down with a cargo of quicksilver and mining supplies on a trip upstream in the fall of 1865, hit a snag and quickly sank. It was only one of nearly 400 steamships to be sunk or stranded between St. Louis and Fort Benton, Montana, during the nineteenth and early twentieth centuries, as they attempted to navigate the treacherous currents of the shallow Missouri River. The remains of the *Bertrand* and its cargo, buried under about thirty feet of mud and sand, were found during the summer of 1967 near the present shoreline of DeSoto Lake.

A number of beaver lodges occur along the edge of the lake, and the cottonwoods and willows on its shore bear mute witness to the beavers' industriousness. Deer tracks lace the newly fallen snow, and coyotes patrol the woods in search of crippled waterfowl. Two fox squirrels temporarily watch the newly arrived geese from a vantage point in a high cottonwood, and then go back to their business of laying in a winter food supply.

Now, in early November, large numbers of geese have already been on the refuge for several weeks. These early migrants have evidently traveled by a more direct route than did the flock that has just come in from Sand Lake. The late arrivals will find little food left within the refuge boundaries. As a result, they will fly daily from ten to thirty miles to cornfields on the broad floodplain of the Missouri, or on the adjoining uplands. Fortunately, the refuge boundaries are sufficiently far from the resting areas that few birds will be gunned down by hunters shooting from highway ditches or private lands on the refuge's perimeter.

Compared with the continuing slaughter at Sand Lake, the refuge at DeSoto Bend provides a welcome respite for Khavik and his family. Together with several hundred thousand other geese, they loiter there most of November. The few degrees of difference in latitude between Sand Lake and DeSoto Bend are

appreciably reflected in the daily temperatures, and rarely does snow completely cover the grainfields for more than a few days. As the month passes on, some of the geese begin to move southward, but these population losses are hardly evident among the seemingly countless birds using the lake. More and more eagles take up residence in the cottonwoods, and they or the coyotes quickly deal with any wounded birds that they find.

Now the geese, although secure and undisturbed within the refuge boundaries, are nearly surrounded by signs of man. Only a few miles to the east, an interstate highway connects the metropolitan areas of Sioux City with the Omaha-Council Bluffs region. A short distance upstream from the refuge, a gigantic new nuclear-power plant is nearly ready to begin operations. What effects the release of its heated waters into the river might have, not only on the river's fish, but also on the wildlife of the adjacent refuge, is an unanswered question. It is one that few of the project's planners bothered to ask.

To the south, the snow geese have a series of potential stopover points arranged like so many stepping stones down the valley of the Missouri. Many of these are areas of rigidly controlled hunting, operated by the game departments of the states concerned. Their use by the geese entails a measure of risk. The next fairly safe stopover point is Squaw Creek National Wildlife Refuge, some eighty air miles south of DeSoto Bend, in northwestern Missouri. It is a mere two-hour flight between these two great refuges, and a certain amount of two-way traffic between them no doubt occurs every year, as weather and foraging conditions might dictate.

Late in the month of November, Khavik and his family join a massive flock of geese departing DeSoto Bend and head southward, flying a thousand feet above the Missouri Valley. Just south of Omaha, they fly over the mouth of the slow-flowing Platte River, which undulates across the state of Nebraska from west to east like a mythical snake-god.

A hundred miles to the west, myriads of sandhill cranes are gathered on the banks of the Platte. Periodically, they tower upward in circles, resembling the gray smoke of a distant prairie fire. Then, when nearly out of sight, they head southward toward Kansas. White-fronted geese are also on the move across the length of the Platte Valley, and hordes of Canada geese are likewise moving southward through the state. The great fall migration through the prairie states is underway.

One autumn day, very long ago, the cranes were preparing to go southward. As they were gathered in a great flock they saw a beautiful young woman standing alone near the village. Admiring her greatly, the cranes gathered about, and lifting her on their widespread wings, bore her far up in the air and away. While the cranes were taking her up they circled below her so closely that she could not fall, and their loud, hoarse cries drowned her calls for help, so she was carried away and never seen again. Ever since that time the cranes always circle about in autumn, uttering their loud cries while preparing to fly southward, as they did at that time.

—Myth of the Eskimos of the Bering Strait Region[1]

CHAPTER 7

The Time of Dead Grass and Frozen Rivers

As THE Missouri River passes southward between southern Nebraska and Iowa, its floodplain encompasses a progressively broader area, gradually merging with the hilly uplands to the west. To the east, the plain abruptly ends a few miles from the river, where a range of wooded loess hills rises sharply about two hundred feet. Between the bases of these eroded, dissected hills and the river itself lies Squaw Creek National Wildlife Refuge, where several small creeks descend the hills and fill a marshy lowland that was once an extensive cordgrass marsh. One of these creeks, Squaw Creek, was reputedly named for the body of a squaw found long ago in an Indian burial scaffold there. The marshy area was once dredged, and attempts were made to drain it for agriculture. These ultimately met with failure, as well as the near destruction of the area's value for waterfowl. However, in 1935 it was designated a national wildlife refuge, primarily for migrating mallards and other ducks.

Originally, snow geese used Squaw Creek only during the spring migration period, but in 1949 the first significant fall use occurred, when 5,500 birds were present. By 1960 their numbers had increased to peak fall populations of 170,000; in 1971, nearly 200,000. Over a ten-year period through 1968 the average peak fall numbers were 96,000 birds; such peak concentrations occur normally in early November, but occasionally as late as early December. Considerable numbers of smaller Canada geese use the refuge on migration, and several thousand large Canada geese usually overwinter there. Likewise, about 100,000 mallards can usually be found through the worst part of the winter, long after snow cover and resulting food shortages have forced the snow geese much farther south.

Squaw Creek is the oldest of the three federal refuges between South Dakota and Missouri that are primarily used by snow geese. It is used long and heavily in the fall by them, and yet hunting pressure here is not nearly so severe as at Sand Lake. In 1970 an estimated 23,440 snow geese were killed around Squaw Creek, and another 4,000 were believed crippled. This figure represents 19 per cent of the peak fall snow goose concentration, and about 6 per cent of the total numbers of snow geese believed to have used the refuge during the entire fall period. This relatively small harvest, as compared to Sand Lake, is probably attributable to the refuge's prohibition of hunting on adjacent highway right-of-ways and the development of private lands for duck rather than goose shooting.[1]

As the snow goose flock approaches the refuge, it scans a largely ice-covered marsh about two miles across and three miles long. Its rim of cattails and bulrushes has taken on the color of burnished copper in the late afternoon sun. The oak- and hickory-covered bluffs abutting the refuge on the east are interrupted in places by almost vertical fissures, which expose the yellowish loess. Red-tailed hawks ride the updrafts along the rim of this palisade, and dozens of bald eagles perch in the cottonwoods beside the marsh or scavenge crippled waterfowl on the ice. In early December, most of the eagles are immatures, the adults having gone to search for fish along the open stretches of the Missouri. Most of the geese, snows and the large Canadas, rest on the ice in the south pool, too far from the reeds to be ambushed by coyotes, and well away from eagle perches. The new arrivals quickly join the others, stopping their downward momentum just above the ice and sliding to a stop at the edge of the resting flock.

By now the geese have consumed much of the corn, rye, and other crops planted for them on the refuge, and they must resort to cattails and bulrushes, or flying to grainfields beyond the refuge boundaries. Each morning cloud after cloud of geese rises from the marsh even before the sun has cleared the forested bluffs of the eastern horizon. Many of them will follow the small tributaries of the Missouri, flying ten or twenty miles to suitable grainfields. Where snow covers the fields, the geese often forage among cattle, on whom they rely to expose the browse or grain. After their morning foraging they fly back to the refuge, spending the day sitting or sleeping on the ice, perhaps taking a late afternoon foraging flight before returning to the refuge to spend the night.

Along the edges of the marsh, raccoons and coyotes search for dead or crippled birds; muskrats and beavers burrow into the levees and dikes; gray and fox squirrels harvest the abundant mast crop. Common in the wooded areas, white-tailed deer may pass below a group of roosting long-eared owls, still resting from a night of hunting. Every evening, following the afternoon feeding session, the geese pour back into the marsh, displacing countless red-winged blackbirds that retire to favored roosting trees. Their numbers are staggeringly large, up to four or five million, supplemented by hordes of starlings until the winter temperatures drive the latter farther south.

As Khavik and his family arrive at Squaw Creek, other geese are already leaving. Many of these are the snow geese that had arrived by a more direct route from Hudson Bay earlier in the fall, and others are small Canada geese from Baffin Island and northern Hudson Bay. Very few of these small Canada geese and white-phase snow geese will follow the Missouri and Mississippi valleys to Louisiana. Instead, they will head almost directly south, cross eastern Kansas, skirt the western edge of the Ozark Plateau and the Ouachita Mountains and follow the valleys of the Sabine and Trinity rivers to the coast of Texas. About half of the blue-phase snow geese using Squaw Creek during fall will winter to the east of the Sabine River in western Louisiana, while the other half will winter farther to the west on the Texas side of the river.

As December—the Moon of the Popping Trees—wears on, the fields around the refuge become more stripped of waste

grain, and the snow covering the adjacent hills creeps ever farther downward into the valley. The ice on the marsh becomes thick enough for coyotes to run across without danger of falling through; eagles constantly watch the duck and goose flocks. A bitter wind funnels down the Missouri Valley, bringing with it the first severe blizzard of the winter. It is once again time to move farther south.

Late in December the snow geese on Squaw Creek refuge detect the change in the weather and begin to depart. After climbing a thousand feet, they head south with the cold north wind at their backs. They cross high above the rolling glacial till plains of northeastern Kansas which, still largely covered by native prairie grasses, support the largest populations of greater prairie chickens remaining in North America. These prairies were also the one-time home of the Kansa Indians, the People of the South Wind. In 1873 the few Kansa Indians who had survived the ravage of smallpox were deported to a reservation in Oklahoma.

Southward over eastern Oklahoma, the Land of the Red Man, the geese fly. Soon they pass over the Ozark Plateau, where the Cherokee Indians of the Carolinas and Georgia were transplanted, and the Ouachita Mountains, where also the Chocktaws of Alabama and Mississippi were placed under the provisions of the Indian Removal Act. These two tribes and the Creek, Chickasaw, and Seminole were the Five Civilized Tribes that were assured these lands in eastern Oklahoma for as long as the grass shall grow and the rivers run. But now the grasses are dead and the rivers frozen, and the geese fly over innumerable oil wells, polluted rivers, and ugly cities.

The goose flock is now over eastern Texas, the original home of the Caddo Indians. The Caddos gave us the name Texas, derived from their word Tejas, meaning friends or allies. At one time these culturally advanced and agriculturally oriented Indians prospered and flourished throughout much of this area, and formed a league called the Haisinai Confederacy. The Caddos were among the first tribes to acquire horses from the Spaniards, and many were killed during the warfare between the Spanish and French during the 1700s. In 1855 the United States Government provided the Caddo Indians with a reservation in the ancestral homeland on the Brazos River, but only a few years later displaced the tribe to southwestern Oklahoma, thus freeing all of eastern Texas for future progress and civilization.

After crossing the Ouachita Mountains, the snow geese need only follow any of the several river systems that flow from that point southeasterly toward the Gulf of Mexico. The Sabine River drainage will lead the birds to the great coastal lowlands of Cameron Parish, Louisiana, and Sabine and Lacassine National Wildlife Refuges. To the east of these is Vermilion Parish, the traditional wintering grounds of the geese that fly directly south from James Bay. To the west, in Texas, are Anahuac, Brazoria, San Bernard, and Aransas National Wildlife Refuges. Connecting these refuges are the marshy coastal flats of Texas, just behind which are the Texas rice fields. The snow geese have finally arrived on their wintering grounds.

A long, long time ago, the goose nation did not migrate south in the autumn, but remained in the land of the Dakotas throughout the winter. Because of the rigors of the winter most of the people of the goose nation perished, so that they were always a small and weak nation. At last one goose had a dream of the southland, that it was pleasant even in winter, that the winter there was mild, and that there was plenty of food there. So she began teaching the other geese that they should practice flying more and thus make their wings strong so that they could fly to the southland before winter. Some people of the goose nation believed the vision and began to practice flying to make their wings strong for the autumn journey. This caused discussion and dissension in the nation, and a law was made which banished the goose that had the vision. She practiced flying all summer and made her wings strong so that in the autumn she was able to fly to the pleasant southland of which she had dreamed. The Mysterious Power which had given her the vision guided her on the long journey and she lived pleasantly through the winter. After the first thunder in the springtime she flew back north to her nation. As always before, many had died during the cold wintertime from the fury of the storms and the scarcity of food. But she told them how pleasantly she had passed the time in the southland, and they saw in what good health she was, so many more of them now believed her vision and her teaching. It was in this way that the geese learned to fly away to the southland in the autumn to escape the storms and cold of winter.

—Teton-Dakota myth[2]

CHAPTER 8

Amid Rice Fields, Salt Marshes, and Bayous

THE COASTAL LOWLANDS and marshes of Louisiana and Texas, which extend almost uninterrupted from the mouth of the Mississippi River on the east to the Rio Grande delta on the Mexico border, provide the most important single waterfowl wintering area in North America. Nearly all of the blue-phase snow geese in North America spend their winter months between Vermilion Bay of Louisiana and Galveston Bay of Texas. From the Louisiana border west along the coast of Texas and south into coastal Mexico are the vast majority of the white-phase lesser snow geese that winter east of the Rocky Mountains. The habitat types of greatest importance to the snow geese in Texas and Louisiana are the tidal marshes and the adjacent native grasslands that have been converted to rice culture.

East of Galveston Bay in Texas, and extending into Louisiana, there occurs a deep-marsh rice belt of fresh, brackish, and saline marshes. These wetlands provide waterfowl with shelter and an abundance of important natural food plants such as salt grass, bulrushes, spike rushes, and widgeon grass. They lie close to the rice fields, which not only offer rice but also smartweeds, wild millet, and pondweeds. In Texas alone these 250,000 wetland acres often support 750,000 ducks and geese during December and January.

West of Galveston Bay and south to Calhoun County, Texas, a shallow-marsh belt replaces the deeper marshes. Spring and fall rains flood the areas between the fresh and tidal marshes, and the waters range from fresh to slightly brackish. Nearby, two million acres are planted with rice, a primary food for some of the wintering waterfowl such as white-fronted geese. Still farther south, from Matagorda Bay to the Rio Grande, a narrow zone of saline marshes nurtures heavy growths of salt grass, cord grass and saltflat-grass. In adjoining bays, rich beds of shoal grass and widgeon grass provide prime foraging areas for wintering redheads, pintails, and scaups. More than a million ducks and nearly half a million geese often winter collectively in the rice belt, coastal marshes, and shallow bays of the lower Texas coast. Snow geese winter most abundantly from Galveston Bay eastward, white-fronted geese concentrate in the rice fields of Colorado and Wharton counties, and Canada geese are most numerous along the middle and lower portions of the Texas coast.[1]

Before the development of a rice economy in Texas, tall native grasses that surrounded the marshes and lined bayous covered its coastal regions. Wide-spreading live oaks, heavily festooned with Spanish moss, lined drainage ways or grew in scattered "motts." Groves of low "shinnery" oaks, locally called "chenieres," grew on sandy ridges. Each spring the haunting booming sounds of the Attwater's prairie chicken once could be heard in all of these coastal prairies all the way from southwestern Louisiana to Cameron County, Texas. But that was in the past. The doom of the Attwater's prairie chicken dates to the Civil War, with the birth of the rice culture in Texas. In 1922, 174,000 acres of rice were planted in coastal Texas; by 1965 this figure had risen to 462,000 acres, as Texas eventually surpassed Louisiana in rice production. Irrigation of the fertile coastal lowlands created ideal land for rice culture, but the natural grasses on which the prairie chickens had depended were gradually destroyed. The discovery of a major oil field in Jefferson County in 1901 led to further habitat destruction; eventually oil wells studded every coastal county in the entire state.[2]

Along the Gulf Coast, current agricultural practice dictates growing rice only every third year, with the fields left fallow or planted to some other crop during the intervening years.

Rice is planted in the spring and raised in flooded fields. The only serious waterfowl crop damage at this time is sometimes caused by fulvous whistling ducks, which may forage on newly sprouted rice in flooded fields. They often pay a heavy penalty for their depredations; insecticides used in coating the seeds to prevent damage from water weevils have sometimes caused extensive mortality to these ducks.[3]

Although snow geese rarely feed on newly planted rice, they forage heavily on shattered rice grains in full stubble, which often remains available to the geese over much of the winter. Canada geese use rice grain to some extent, but prefer corn, which is more prevalent from Lavaca Bay southward. Where neither corn nor rice is cultivated, the geese may forage in sorghum fields, or sometimes consume flax shoots. However, the snow geese are basically marsh-feeders, preferring to grub in the mud for plant roots and stalks, and normally forage in the uplands during wet weather.[4]

Formerly in Louisiana, the blue-phase snow geese rarely strayed far from the coastal marshes and were almost never more than eight miles from salt beaches. Except for a relatively small population associated with the mouth of the Mississippi River, the majority concentrated in the 85 miles between the east end of Marsh Island and the mouth of the Mermentau River. Here they foraged on a variety of native foods, including the seeds of feather grass and wild millet, the roots of bulrushes and cord grass, and to some extent, the roots and tubers of duck potato.[5]

Since the 1930s, the geese of Louisiana have altered their foraging behavior and winter distribution patterns considerably. Now the snow geese winter almost exclusively in the rice fields, cattle pastures, and other agricultural lands. The development of high snow goose usage of rice fields occurred later in Louisiana than in Texas, but the wintering behavior of Canada geese in Louisiana has changed even more drastically in recent years. These geese originally were associated with tidal marshes, much like the snow geese, but increasingly became birds of the coastal farmlands and cattle ranges. In recent years large numbers have been wintering in more northerly states such as Missouri and

Illinois, and now many never reach their traditional Louisiana wintering areas.[6] Nevertheless, recent winter surveys in Louisiana indicate that between 300,000 and 400,000 geese usually still winter in the state. Of these 80 per cent are snow geese, and the remainder are mostly white-fronted geese. Additionally, Louisiana harbors close to five million ducks each winter. About a million of these are pintails, and a half million or more each of mallards, gadwalls, baldpates, and green-winged teal are often present.

Until recently no federal sanctuaries for waterfowl existed in Texas east of Galveston Bay, although this area is of critical importance to wintering snow geese. The establishment in 1963 of the 9,800-acre Anahuac National Wildlife Refuge altered the situation. East of this refuge, starting at the Texas-Louisiana border, is the 143,000-acre Sabine National Wildlife Refuge, and just beyond is the 32,000-acre Lacassine National Wildlife Refuge. Several other major sanctuaries of importance to snow geese also occur along the coastline of southwestern Louisiana. These include the 88,000-acre Rockefeller Foundation Wildlife Sanctuary and the 28,000-acre Paul J. Rainey Wildlife Sanctuary. The state of Louisiana has also set aside the entire 79,000 acres of Marsh Island as a game preserve.

These vital refuges provide protection for most of the snow geese wintering between Galveston and Vermilion bays. Between these bays not only are there more than half a million wintering snow geese, but also nearly two million dabbling ducks. Half a million scaups also winter along the Louisiana coast, 10,000 canvasbacks flock to Wax Lake east of Vermilion Bay, and 15,000 ring-necked ducks gather on the Mississippi River delta to the east. It is a winter concentration of waterfowl without parallel in North America.[7]

Anahuac Refuge deceives the average observer. From ground level an unlimited vista of grasses and sedges is broken only by occasional rows of ancient salt cedar trees planted by early ranchers and farmers. Yet, a bird approaching from above sees that the grasses and sedges are often awash in a sea of shallow water. Irrigation drainage ditches and natural inlets, or "guts," connect the refuge with the adjoining eastern branch of Galveston Bay. About 10 per cent of the refuge's total acreage is cultivated in rice, millet, and upland crops for wildlife consumption. Additionally, "water farming" is practiced to encourage the growth of natural food plants. In this process, fields that have been grazed by cattle are burned, disked, and then flooded, stimulating the growth of millet and associated waterfowl foods. Crayfish and other crustaceans enter the flooded fields, providing abundant food for herons, egrets, and similar waders.

In the nearby waters of East Bay, flocks of white pelicans, cormorants, loons, and mergansers work the tidal shallows for fish. Turkey vultures gracefully ride the thermals above the refuge, and an occasional alligator floats motionless on the marshy waters. The refuge protects the extremely rare red wolf, which has been almost completely eliminated from the rest of its once broad range.[8] Confusion between the red wolf and the smaller coyote, as well as some interbreeding between them, makes the status of the red wolf very difficult to judge. However, the population of the larger and more typically wolflike form apparently numbers only in the hundreds, and several of the animals use Anahuac Refuge as a protected foraging area.

For Khavik, Khanguk, and their two offspring, the first part of December passes uneventfully. They remain within the boundaries of Anahuac Refuge, seeking out the remaining stands of rice and millet. They leisurely and efficiently strip the millet plants of their large seed clusters. Grasping the stems as close to the seed heads as possible, they pull the plant down by taking a few steps, and move their bills up to a point just below the seed cluster. Holding their heads to one side, the birds move their heads quickly upward and backward, pulling the grass stem between the closed mandibles. The seeds are simultaneously stripped from the stem and packed against the upper side of the bill. When the bill is opened, the seeds fall directly into the goose's mouth.

December marks the first of the courtship flights of the snow geese. Birds that are somewhat over a year old are now attaining sexual maturity, even though most of them will not attempt to breed until their third year. For them, winter and spring are a time for prolonged aerial chases and aquatic courtship and the forging of pair bonds that may last a lifetime.

In courting flights two or more males chase a single female, with the strongest or most favored male attempting to stay directly behind the female. As in aerial courtship by ducks, a male may even try to grasp the female's tail with his bill, and both birds call constantly. It is not known to what extent the female may actively solicit such chases, or whether she is simply forced into them by the press of so many attentive males. In any case, a single male eventually succeeds in establishing social dominance over his competitors and successfully keeps all other competing males away from the female. Perhaps, as with ducks, the female may show a definite preference for a particular male by responding differentially to him, but there is not the formalized and complex social courtship typical of most duck species. Instead, the female seems simply to accept the fact that a single male has assumed the responsibility of protecting her from the constant advances of other males. When she regularly performs a "triumph ceremony" with him after his return from threatening or attacking some opponent, the pair-bonding process is achieved.[9]

While the yearling snow geese are finding mates, those hatched during the previous breeding season are themselves undergoing some marked external changes. By early to mid-January, some of the blue-phase juveniles develop a white "frosting" on their otherwise dark heads, and the slate-gray body tints typical of young white-phase birds gradually disappear, remaining longest on the scapulars and upper wing coverts. The last major remnant of the juvenile plumage, the grayish secondary feathers, will persist until the midsummer molt.

As December passes, the numbers of geese using Anahuac Refuge increases, while the food resources within the refuge boundaries diminish. More and more time is spent foraging, and a larger proportion of the birds fly out beyond the refuge to seek rice fields still containing waste grain or germinating green plants in the stubble. Bordering the refuge to the east is a duck and goose "hunting preserve" that is considerably larger than the refuge itself. Here, sportsmen can rent a blind and join in the killing of the tens of thousands of geese and ducks that are shot on private hunting preserves each year in Texas. In three recent years this ranch has annually entertained over 5,000 hunters, for a general admission fee of only eight dollars a day (five for children under sixteen). Here private individuals gain personal profit from a resource that belongs to all North Americans, and wealthy businessmen who know little more about hunting than the general direction in which to point their shotguns are treated to the dubious pleasures of shooting birds out of the sky for only a small daily fee, often tax-deductible. Many of these operations charge twenty to twenty-five dollars a day for such "sportsmen," providing decoys, blinds, and expert guides. The hunters provide the money and a willingness to shoot at anything that comes within range.

The geese cannot distinguish a rice field littered with white cardboard decoys from one in which wild geese are peacefully foraging. When Khavik, Khanguk, and their young approach the field, their memories of Sand Lake remain unaroused. But, several birds in the flock having recently been exposed to gunfire, the group repeatedly circles the field, scanning every foot of its surface for a poorly concealed blind or unusual movements. However, they see only decoys and hear the imploring calls of a goose that has just recognized one of its family members emanating from a hidden pit. Their suspicions allayed, the geese make a final sweep downwind, then turn back into the wind with their wings cupped, their tails spread, and their feet lowered. Suddenly, there is a shout of "Now!" Simultaneously three pits appear among the decoys, from each of which a human figure emerges. With a deafening barrage of gunfire, the scene is suddenly one of dead and dying geese plummeting toward earth. Among them is Khanguk. Hit by a dozen pellets in her head and body, she dies instantly. Yet, Khavik and his two youngsters remain unscathed, and, before the hunters can reload, frantically climb out of shotgun range. While the two young birds flee toward the refuge, Khavik circles high over-head, calling wildly. But there is no answer from below; only the crumpled and lifeless bodies of six geese lie strewn among the decoys. His calls unanswered, Khavik finally turns back toward the refuge. His mate of two years is now gone, and he will have little opportunity to remate prior to the spring flight northward. Now, the only course left for him is to rejoin his two surviving young and to lead them safely back to the breed-ing grounds. In another year they will be ready to mate and, should he live that long, he too might acquire a new mate.*

* The loss of one member of a pair probably occurs quite frequently. The annual mortality rate of this population of adult lesser snow geese has been estimated by Hugh Boyd as 37 per cent. The resulting probability of a pair losing one of its members through death during the course of a twelve-month period is, therefore, 46 per cent, and there is a 14 per cent probability that both members of the pair will die. The odds are thus less than one to one (40 per cent to 60 per cent) that both members of a pair will survive a twelve-month period. Even asuming a somewhat lower annual adult mortality rate of 25 per cent, as is suggested by banding studies of lesser snow geese on the Pacific coast, the odds of both members of a pair surviving for at least twelve months are only slightly better than one to one.[10]

One third of a million blue and snow geese were shot annually by U.S. hunters in the Mississippi and Central Flyways during the late 1960s. Kills by licensed hunters in Canada only accounted for about a tenth of this number. Judging from recoveries of snow geese banded by Graham Cooch at South-ampton Island, Texas hunters were responsible for the largest proportion of birds harvested from the Southampton flock. In the nine-year period between 1962 and 1970, the annual Texas and Louisiana blue and snow goose kill averaged about 89,000 and 78,000 birds, or more than half of the total U.S. kill in the Central and Mississippi Flyways. Yet, in spite of this disproportionately high wintering-ground kill, hunters from Texas and Louisiana have recently accused federal refuges of practicing techniques that tend to hold the birds in more northerly states for longer periods during fall, thus depriving the south-ern hunters of their traditional share of the annual goose slaughter.[11]

In the fall of 1972, after a disastrous breeding season in the Canadian arctic the estimated total wintering snow goose population in the Central and Missis-sippi Flyways was down almost 23 per cent from the previous year. This substantial population reduction, reflecting the combination of a minimal breeding success and increased goose-hunting pressures (North Dakota re-ported the third highest goose kill in history), resulted in recommendations for a decrease in hunting limits to four snow geese daily in both flyways.

The geese and ducks were created before there was any water on the surface of the earth. They wanted water so as to be able to swim and dive as was their nature, but Aba objected and said he would not allow water on the earth as it was dangerous, and he then said to the geese and ducks: "What is the good of water, and why do you want it?" And together they answered "We want it to drink on hot days." Then Aba asked how much water they wanted and the ducks replied: "We want a great deal of water; we want swamps and rivers and lakes to be scattered all over the surface of the earth. And also we want grass and moss to grow in the water, and frogs and snakes to live there."

Aba asked the geese and ducks why they wanted frogs and snakes to live in the water and they answered that frogs and snakes were their food, and they told Aba how they

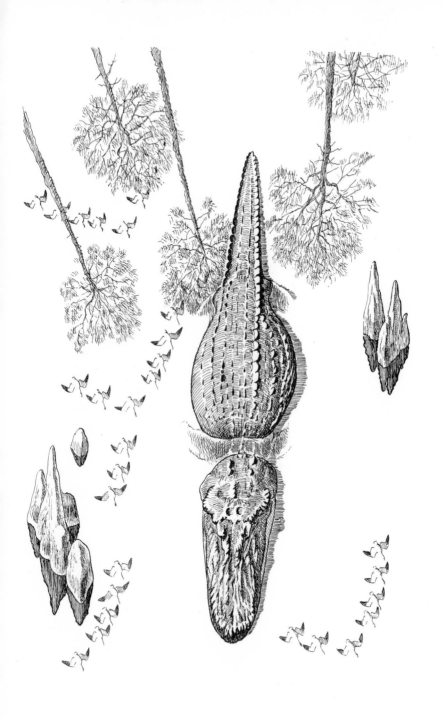

could dive and swim beneath the water and catch them. And then Aba told them how he had made the sun, the air, and the earth and asked if that was not enough. "No," was the reply of all, "we want water."

The alligators then spoke to Aba and likewise asked for water. The alligators told of their desire to live in dark places, deep in the waters of bayous, among the roots of cypress and black gum trees, for there the water was the best.

Aba then spoke to all saying he would give them all the water they desired, but that he had talked with them to hear what they would have to say.

And even now the ducks and geese claim the swamps and marshes.

—Choctaw myth[12]

CHAPTER 9

The Land of Flat Waters

Behold also my wings.
The feathers of my wings the little ones shall use as plumes.
When they use the feathers of my wings as plumes,
The days of cloudless skies
Shall always be at their command as they travel the path of life.
The four great divisions of the days
They shall always be able to reach as they travel the path of life.

—Chant of the Great White Swan, Osage Indian Rite[1]

BETWEEN THE Red River of the South, which forms most of the boundary between Oklahoma and Texas, and the Niobrara River, which cuts across the northern edge of Nebraska, a series of east-west-oriented rivers meanders across the Great Plains toward the Missouri and Mississippi rivers like ancient bison trails. Many of these rivers served as natural routes for the early explorers and settlers to follow westward across the plains, and formed the basis for such routes as the Oregon and Mormon trails. For waterfowl migrating northward, these river valleys still offer a number of stopover points situated at intervals that can be easily crossed in a flight of only a few hours. The Platte River (from the French "plat," meaning flat) and its adjoining wetlands is one of the most important of these stopover points.

The Platte River moves leisurely across Nebraska (from the Oto's "Nebrathka," or "flat water"), inches deep in some years and overflowing its low banks in others. Its channels are unpredictable from one year to the next, with silty bars and islands forming and eroding away at random. If the islands persist long enough, dense growth of willows and red osier dogwoods eventually grows up and stabilizes them, providing excellent cover for deer, pheasants, and quails. Until then, the bars and islands offer abundant resting places for migrating waterfowl, which begin to move into the Platte Valley in late February and reach peak concentrations during the second half of March. By mid-April they have nearly abandoned the Platte for more northerly staging areas.

To the north of the Platte River lies the Nebraska sandhills, a vast near-wilderness of natural grasses resting gently on an ocean of sand dunes that were deposited during late glacial times. To the south and east of the sandhills are the undulating loess plains of eastern Nebraska, wind-deposited soils that were blown in from the sandhills region and from glacial outwash areas. Situated amid this loess plain to the south of the Platte Valley is the rainwater basin of Nebraska. Extending over ten counties and containing nearly 4,000 square miles, this area consists of closed drainage systems that empty into depressions of from less than an acre to more than 1,000 acres in size. A layer of clay prevents rapid subsurface drainage, and during wet years the basins become flooded and converted into shallow marshes that are lined with cattails, bulrushes, and smartweeds. They thus provide food and sanctuary for migratory waterfowl and in favorable years may serve as a nesting habitat.[2]

In early March, Khavik and his two offspring leave their winter quarters as part of a massive goose flock taking advantage of a south wind and a clear sky, crossing the high plains of eastern Texas during the evening hours. During the night they fly over eastern Oklahoma, and skirt the eastern edge of the Flint Hills of Kansas. On these native grasslands greater prairie chickens are already assembled on their hilltop booming grounds, waiting for the first rays of dawn to begin their display. Many of their booming grounds are still good places to look for arrowheads, clear evidence that the current use of these display sites represents the unbroken transmission of avian traditions backward over hundreds of generations to presettlement times.

As the sun begins to rise above the eastern horizon, both the prairie chickens and the snow geese are bathed in its golden light. Many of the geese turn easterly into the sun and head for Squaw Creek National Wildlife Refuge. However, it is usually filled to capacity with snow geese that have moved in earlier from wintering areas in western Louisiana. These early arrivals have a much higher incidence of blue-phase birds than do the flocks that are now moving up from Texas. Many that wintered in Louisiana have fresh gold to orange stains on their faces, which they acquired from grubbing in the Louisiana marshes.

As if recognizing the fact that the nearly quarter million geese already present at Squaw Creek have made serious inroads on the available food supplies there, Khavik and his family remain in a flock that continues northward along the valley of the Big Blue River. As they cross into Nebraska they pass over the Homestead National Monument, where Daniel Freeman staked out one of the first land claims under the provisions of the Homestead Act of 1862. The passage of this legislation marked the decline of the natural grasslands of the Great Plains, and the start of the homesteading era.

It is past sunrise when the goose flock finally drops into a large marsh in Clay County, not far from Harvard. The snow geese there are a small minority of the total geese using the marsh, which are predominantly white-fronted and Canada geese. Sharing the marshy lowlands with the geese are hundreds of sandhill cranes, while great flocks of mallards and pintails forage in the marsh and the adjacent grainfields. The marsh is a bedlam of sounds, with those of the cranes and the geese predominating. This marsh represents one of the easternmost of the concentration areas of the white-fronted geese, for which the Platte Valley is the most important spring staging area between their Texas wintering grounds and their Canadian breeding areas. Within three months, the cranes and geese sharing this valley will have spread out over the North American arctic from Baffin Island to Alaska, and some of the cranes may even continue on into Siberia before stopping to nest.

Twenty miles to the northwest is the Platte River, whose channels are filled with meltwaters from snows that fell in Colorado and Wyoming, and with bars and islands that are teeming with sandhill cranes which have recently arrived from New Mexico. Each spring 200,000 sandhill cranes gather along a 150-mile stretch of this river in central Nebraska. These flocks comprise about 60 per cent of the total North American crane population and represent the world's largest congregation of sandhill cranes. Nearly half of the total population of the rare greater sandhill crane are among them. The even rarer whooping crane has also traditionally used the Platte River as one of its major stopover points between Canada and Texas. The river also provides shelter for nearly 150,000 white-fronted geese each spring, or about 85 per cent of this species' mid-continent population. Large numbers of Canada geese and a few snow geese roost on the river. Through March, mallards, pintails, and green-winged teals perform their exciting courtship flights above its broad expanse, and small flotillas of common mergansers navigate the faster and deeper channels. Bald eagles patrol its length, and coyotes silently stalk its brushy shorelines.

This unique and irreplaceable wildlife heritage will soon be destroyed if the Bureau of Reclamation diverts this part of the Platte to provide additional irrigation water for a few farmers, whose pumping activities have been depleting the area's groundwater supplies more rapidly than they can be naturally replenished. If the Mid-State Project is carried out, for several critical months this stretch of the river will be reduced to a dry stream bed, and the waterfowl, fish, furbearers, and big game that depend on it will be displaced or eliminated.[3] The cost to American taxpayers for this political boondoggle and ecological disaster will be at least 130 million dollars, while the agricultural benefits will only amount to 4.5 million dollars per year following the project's completion. The wildlife losses cannot be so easily calculated. One can estimate the direct losses to hunters, fishermen, and trappers in terms of lost opportunities for their activities. But what is the monetary value of a March sky laced with geese? Who can place a currency figure on a gray cloud of cranes riding so high that they are finally lost to sight and only their voices persist, drifting downward in a wild chorus of excitement? Is the sweet spring scent of a plum thicket in bloom a treasure of the mind or of the pocketbook? Who can program the sights, sounds, and smells of a Platte Valley spring into a computer analysis designed to analyze questions in terms of black or white, yes or no, plus or minus? What, indeed, are the worths of a wild river running full, of birds flying free, or of a human spirit renewed in the presence of these wonders? Politicians speak of defending freedom around the world and simultaneously encourage the degradation and destruction of freedom for our own wildlife and, ultimately, for all of us.

For the geese and cranes, the Platte River is the center of existence. Each day before dawn the cranes begin to take flight from their roosts in the middle of the river where they have stood in the shallow waters all night long, safe from coyotes and other disturbance. By sunrise most of the cranes have flown to the moist meadows near the river, or to fields of winter wheat, corn or milo, where they forage for waste grain, green plants, and the few insects that are to be found. In another hour or two they are joined by the geese, which together with the pintails and mallards concentrate on cornfields and generally avoid close association with the cranes. By midday the ducks and geese have usually returned to the safety of the river, while the cranes forage in a leisurely fashion all day long. By the latter part of the afternoon the geese and ducks may again leave the river for a second foraging period, but by then the first of the cranes are returning to their roosts. Clearing the trees that line the river by a hundred yards or more of altitude, the cranes circle their roosting areas and gracefully spiral downward to land on the adjacent islands and bars. They will remain there, preening and resting, until they finally wade out into the river after dark.

As the sun glows red in the west, the sky is strewn with skeins of cranes headed for the river. Here and there are flocks of geese as well, but many of these will wait until after sunset before heading back to roost. The cranes already on the roosting areas set up a clamor that is answered by the approaching birds, and their rolling, musical calls echo up and down the length of the river. The chorus grows to a crescendo with sunset and slowly subsides as the reddish glow on the western horizon darkens to purple and finally to black. By then, the river is quiet, giving the same peace and protection that it gave to America's pioneers more than a century earlier and to uncounted generations of Indians who have camped on its shorelines for thousands of years. The river is the touchstone of Nebraska's history and the lifeblood of her people and wildlife. To purposefully destroy it would be an abdication of historical perspective and of ecological responsibility.

In the rainwater basin, Khavik and his offspring continue to share a lagoon with a mixed flock of several thousand snow, Canada, and white-fronted geese. In this meeting place of eastern and western faunas, the dawns are heralded by both eastern and western meadowlarks, and the flickers vary in color from yellow-shafted to red-shafted and all intermediate shades. Each day new waterfowl arrivals appear on the marsh. Brown and grayish gadwalls now may be seen here and there, and American wigeons are suddenly everywhere, skimming over the water in frantic courtship flights and swimming near the redheads in the event that a succulent pondweed frond might be stolen from an unwary bird. The redheads too are actively courting, and their distinctive soft and catlike calls carry for surprising distances over the marsh. However, the rattling, wooden calls of the newly arrived shovelers fade in the hubbub of the marsh, while the hollow pumping sounds of courting American bitterns betray their recent arrival. Killdeers periodically scream in the distance, and a marsh hawk silently courses just above the cattails and smartweeds. In the distance, a red-tailed hawk lazily circles in the blue sky, and from even farther away the ethereal melody of migrating cranes gives voice to the fact that spring has arrived in Nebraska. As if to prove it, the mellow *curleeuuu* notes of a long-billed curlew on the way to its sandhills nesting grounds penetrate the air, and a series of *tseel* whistles reveal the arrival of the season's first blue-winged teal. The ahihidtu of the Omaha Indians, the blue-winged teal was the betrayer duck in the myth of the Haxegi. Like the curlew and swan, it also appeared in the Osage Indians' peace ceremony, and their voices assured the hearer that he would also walk in peace and safety.

At that very time and place,

He, the great white swan, was heard to say,

When, in appeal, he was called to, in this wise: "Ho! grandfather,

The little ones have no means by which to control the sky."

Then, in the distance he was heard to make reply, saying: "Ho! little ones,

You have said the little ones have no means by which to control the sky.

I shall be the means by which the little ones can control the sky.

Behold, the whiteness of my body,

And behold the whiteness, the purity of the sky,

Verily, I am a person who has made himself to resemble the sky in purity.

When the little ones make of me the means by which to control the sky

They shall be able, through their life's journey, to make the god of the upper region

To lie in perfect purity."

—Osage Peace Ceremony[4]

CHAPTER 10

To the Land Where the Rivers Run North

The Coyote said, "I will paint [the world] with blood. There shall be blood in the world; and people shall be born there, having blood. There shall be birds born who shall have blood. Everything—all things shall have blood that are to be created in this world. And in another place, making it red, there shall be red rocks. It will be as if blood were mixed up with the world, and thus the world will be beautiful."

—Maidu myth[1]

UNLIKE THE SITUATION only a few hundred miles farther north, the weather in Nebraska can improve with remarkable swiftness, from a frigid cold to a summery hot spell. The snows deposited by a storm on one day can be gone only a few days later, under the heat of the ever-increasing angle of the sun's rays during early April. The cranes of the Platte Valley have felt the change, and their numbers have gradually declined as flock after flock has taken wing and disappeared over the rolling dunes of the Nebraska sandhills. The skies over the Platte are no longer filled with the fluty notes of courting pintails, and the laughing sounds of the white-fronted geese have become only a memory.

In the rainwater basin, increasing numbers of blue-winged teals and ruddy ducks are now arriving. The male teals are radiant in their newly acquired nuptial plumage, while most of the male ruddies still carry traces of the dull winter plumage. However, a few already have the cobalt-blue bill color of the breeding adults and are swimming about with vertically cocked tails. Many of the teals will remain here to nest, together with pintails, shovelers, mallards, gadwalls, and a few ruddy ducks. But for the snow geese, together with the green-winged teals, wigeons and most of the diving ducks, it is time to depart for more northerly points.

As the geese cross the drift plains of northeastern Nebraska, they look down on a landscape of soft pastels and muted earth tones—gold where harvested grainfields of the previous autumn still stand unplowed, black and green where rows of winter wheat make delicate tracings on the rich loam soil. Near rivers and creeks, the lifeless winter gray of willows and cottonwoods have been transformed into a hazy golden green, while the oaks on the hills remain a somber brown. Snow still laces ravines and marks the north sides of farm groves, and ice chunks occasionally float down the rivers. As the plains sweep to the west, they take on a bluer cast, until they merge imperceptibly with the distant horizon. The open water of the ponds below reflects the spring sky as if it were a carpet of blue; the white backs of male goldeneyes, scaups, and common mergansers twinkle like tiny stars in the March sunshine.

As the flock approaches the Missouri River between Sioux City and Yankton, many of its members drop into the bottomlands near Volin, South Dakota, one of the major spring staging areas in southeastern South Dakota. Others, including Khavik and his offspring, follow the small valley marking the course of the Big Sioux River. The snow geese follow this wooded valley, forming the boundary between South Dakota and northwestern Iowa, northward over brushy ravines and contoured terraces that from the air resemble ripples on a frozen ocean. Roads at mile intervals crisscross the land, and farm groves pepper the landscape for as far as the eye can see. Toward the east occasional outcrop boulders of reddish quartzite dot the prairie like giant drops of blood. To this "Country of Peace," near the headwaters of the Rock and Pipestone rivers, came many tribes of Plains Indians to quarry the precious reddish rocks that they needed for making calumets or peace pipes. The first white man to describe accurately this area and its associated legends was George Catlin, who reached the Pipestone region in 1836.

As Catlin noted, the Dakotas believed that, before the creation of man, the Great Spirit used to slay bison and eat them on the ledge of the rocks at the top of the Coteau des Prairies. The bisons' blood, running over the rocks, turned them red. The Dakotas also believed that at one time, when all the tribes were warring, the Great Spirit called them together at the place of the red stones. After the people had gathered, the Great Spirit stood at the top of the rocks and from a piece of the red stone fashioned a large pipe. Smoking it, He told the multitudes that the pipe was part of their flesh, and even though they were at war they must meet at this place as friends, to quarry the stone. From this stone they too could make the calumets with which they could appease the Great Spirit and find peace. A century later, the quarries lie largely abandoned, the Dakotas are scattered and mostly confined to reservations, and this once-sacred site is an air-conditioned tourist attraction for middle-class Americans.

North of Sioux Falls, the snow geese leave the valley of the Big Sioux on a more westerly heading. The nearly waterless land to the east is the Missouri Coteau des Prairies area. More snow lines the ravines, and little green is to be seen in the fields. Snow also lies deeper in the shelter belts, each of which, in contrast to the small farm groves of Nebraska, stretches for a quarter mile or more along the country roads. The birds must soon land and wait for spring to catch up with them. A few miles west of Brookings there begins a chain of shallow lakes and marshes that stretches northward to the North Dakota line. For the snow geese, the traditional stopping point in this chain is Lake Preston, just west of Brookings. Lake Preston is only about a hundred miles south of Sand Lake and Lake Traverse. The area lying within the triangle formed by these three points represents the finest waterfowl habitat in all of South Dakota. This area includes Waubay National Wildlife Refuge (from the

Dakota language, meaning "place of birds hatching"), in the heart of South Dakota's waterfowl breeding grounds.

The snow geese approach Lake Preston, still partly frozen. Earlier arrivals dot its icy surface. Setting their wings while still a thousand feet above the lake, the birds quickly lose altitude. Remaining in flight formation, they parachute downward almost vertically, as the birds already on the lake broadcast a deafening chorus of greeting notes. Around the flock of resting geese a swarm of mallards and pintails stands massed like troops guarding royalty. The mallards are mostly adult males, and the few females are incessantly engaged in courtship flights around the edges of the lake. Pintails are present in slightly smaller numbers, and along the margins of the ice goldeneyes and mergansers bob about in the frigid waters. Periodically, a splash of water and a sharp *zee-at* note marks the location of a displaying male goldeneye, as it throws its head sharply backward and simultaneously kicks water up behind. The distinctive mellow calls of the male pintails provide a background pizzicato to the constant din of the snow geese, while the reedy notes of the male mallards are lost in the uproar of sound. Along the edges of the lake the earliest of the arriving male red-winged blackbirds are already starting to claim their territories, and western meadowlarks on the adjoining hillsides are doing the same. Overhead, Lapland longspurs are moving northward in great flocks, their weak tinkling calls inaudible in the general commotion.

In the Dakotas, winter releases its grip grudgingly, but when it finally does so the changes each day become almost palpable. There is a quickening of the senses, and the arrival of each new spring bird migrant adds a new dimension almost daily to the beauty of the season. The days are born crisp and cold, with thin layers of ice appearing on ponds that barely had become fully thawed the day before, but by midday the ice is again gone and the blue skies of spring are again reflected from the water's surface. Looking upward, the watchful eye can detect skeins of waterfowl cleaving their way farther northward at altitudes nearly beyond the limits of human detection, and on glancing downward the first insects of the season can be seen moving sluggishly about, as if somehow dimly aware that the winter is at long last over.

The geese remain at Lake Preston for a little more than a week, for the winds of spring are now blowing more strongly, and the daytime temperatures thaw the ice much more rapidly than the nighttime ones refreeze it. Harvested cornfields which have been covered with snow for five months are now exposed, providing an abundant food supply. It is a two-hour flight from Lake Preston to their next staging area, and so the birds take flight. The majority of the snow geese will fly to Sand Lake, but, as if remembering their experiences there the previous fall, Khavik and his two young take a more easterly course. Soon they are within sight of Big Stone Lake, which from the air looks like a wide river that lies in a broad valley and is oriented in a northwest-to-southeast direction. Just beyond is the similarly shaped Lake Traverse, which is in a southwest-to-northeast orientation. Between them is the Big Stone Moraine, a ridge of rounded hills that rise to about 1,200 feet and once produced the impoundment that was to become glacial Lake Agassiz. The city of Browns Valley is close to the point at which this great impoundment first broke through its confines and began to cut a gorge through Big Stone Moraine. As the waters of the lake rushed through this outlet channel, erosion allowed the levels of Lake Agassiz to drop nearly 100 feet in a series of stages. Eventually the lake level became almost stabilized when the outlet was being eroded through bedrock. Finally, retreat of glacial ice farther north exposed new Canadian outlets for the lake, drying up the southern outlet and gradually draining the lake bed. Today, Lake Traverse remains as the last vestige of the torrent that once flowed south through Big Stone Moraine. From this point on, the waters all flow north.[2]

As the geese fly over Lake Traverse, they are blind to the evidence of its geological history. They know it only as a traditional resting place, and already its ice-free areas are jammed with ducks and geese. For the waterfowl, Lake Traverse and Big Stone Lake represent the northernmost point in the eastern

Dakotas that the birds can reach in early spring and be assured of both food and reasonable protection from the elements. To the north, the fertile and marshless agricultural croplands of the Red River Valley stretch far away toward Canada. The valley is as flat and barren as a billiard table, its surface features broken only by the woodlands of the river itself, and the monotonous, regular crosswork pattern of the section roads.

Mixed among the ducks and geese on Lake Traverse is a flock of whistling swans, recently arrived from their Chesapeake Bay wintering grounds. Having flown nearly 1,500 miles in an almost westerly direction, they are ready to start heading on a more northerly course. Some of these birds have breeding-ground destinations as far away as the Anderson and Mackenzie river deltas, some 3,000 miles from Chesapeake Bay. Like the snow geese, they are halfway home.[3]

For as long as the waterfowl have used the Lake Traverse area as a spring and fall concentration area, Indians have camped along its shores and hunted the abundant waterfowl. A Dakota village, *Ptansinta* (Tails of the Otter), was located at the head of the lake. A large glacial boulder found northwest of Browns Valley, and now located in a park in the city, is one of several such boulders incised with petroglyphs that have been found in the area. Marked with two handlike markings, it was considered by the Dakotas to represent the footprints of the Thunder Bird. In their traditions they believed that a small cloud once rose upward from behind the hills west of Lake Traverse and Big Stone Lake. It was the Thunder Bird, or *Wakinyan,* which lived among the lakes to the west. The flapping of its wings caused the crashing of the thunder, and flames of lightning issued forth from its nostrils. As it flew, the heavens darkened and the rain fell in torrents. Finally, the Thunder Bird stopped to rest on the ridge of hills a few miles west of the south end of Lake Traverse, and on alighting on a large granite boulder it left the imprints of its feet on the boulder's surface. Thus the rock became sacred or *wakan*, and was regarded by the Dakotas as the everlasting resting place of the Thunder Bird. Not far west of Lake Traverse are a number of small lakes called

Wakinyan oye, or the place of thunderer's track. Farther northwest, across the North Dakota line, is Tewaukon National Wildlife Refuge (possibly from the Dakota's *khe-wakan*, on sacred hill), another important stopping point for migrating geese.[4]

Like Lake Preston, Lake Traverse and Sand Lake are shortterm stopover points for the geese in spring. They must follow the retreating winter as rapidly as possible, in order to reach their breeding grounds just as their nesting areas are emerging from their winter snow cover. Having arrived at Lake Traverse the first week of April, they are ready to leave by the third. Now they set their course for Devils Lake. Like the stopover points farther south, it is surrounded by grainfields that provide abundant supplies of food, while the extensive lake surface provides protection and freedom from disturbance. However, the less saline lakes to the north of Devils Lake, such as Lac Aux Morts and Sweetwater Lake, are more attractive to the geese and are used by them more heavily.

The snow geese spend much of the last half of April and early May in this part of northeastern North Dakota, their center of abundance being in the vicinity of Lac Aux Morts, but spreading out as far west as the Souris River. These more westerly flocks will fly over the Turtle Mountains and regather in the Whitewater Lake area of southwestern Manitoba. These predominantly white-phase birds are probably headed for breeding almost directly to the north. However, Khavik and his young join the flocks that will concentrate between Winnipeg and Whitewater Lake. In the 1930s the greatest single concentration area was in the vicinity of Grants Lake, near Meadow, Manitoba, according to J. Dewey Soper. He believed that as many as four or five million geese concentrated there each spring, and reported earlier estimates of up to fifty million birds. These estimates were either wildly optimistic, or the mid-continent population of snow geese must have declined greatly in recent decades. In recent years the major spring staging areas have been in the Pembina River Valley, mainly between Morden and Cartwright, and extending southward into northern North Dakota. The most reliable recent estimates of the numbers of snow geese using this area during spring are those of Hans Blockpoel, who concluded on the basis of personal observations and radar information that between 650,000 and one million geese were present in 1970. Most midwinter inventories made by federal biologists in the late 1960s indicated well under a million snow geese in the entire Central and Mississippi Flyways, but in 1971 a more realistic total of 1,340,000 birds was reported to be present. Thus, a million birds, or nearly all of the snow geese of the two flyways, must concentrate in the northern North Dakota and southern Manitoba area each spring.

The prairies, croplands, and marshes of southern Manitoba provide the last resting place for the snow geese prior to their passage over the coniferous forests that form a broad belt between that area and Hudson Bay. It is a minimum flight distance of 500 miles between Winnipeg and York Factory, which lies at the mouth of the Nelson River on the west coast of Hudson Bay. Between these two points the landscape is pitted with deep lakes and scarred with the rocky outcrops of the Canadian Shield; the forests have barely begun to hide the scouring effects of the last glacier. The lakes and streams of the area are poor in nutrients and have few edible plants so that leaving the lush croplands and marshes of southern Manitoba is the start of the reproductive stresses for the geese. In addition, the more northerly latitude of York Factory and the influence of the frozen expanse of adjacent Hudson Bay mean that the geese will be flying from the pleasant mid-spring conditions of southern Canada into the chilling cold of late winter on the tundra. But there can be no hesitation; the birds must beat spring to the Arctic.

It is now mid-May. For more than a week the weather has been poor, with frequent rain and heavy cloud cover. As the weather slowly begins to improve, the wind moves from an easterly to a northerly direction. By late afternoon the birds begin taking off in groups of a few hundred. They rise to an altitude of 1,300 feet, then strike out in a northeasterly direction. By sunset the departure rate has swelled, and the flocks soon cross over the Winnipeg area in a broad front at least 100 miles wide. For the next two days the geese continue to leave their staging grounds, with the later birds taking a more northerly course and probably heading for breeding grounds on the northern coast of Keewatin. Less than 48 hours after the departure of the first birds, the last have also gone, and the prairies of southern Manitoba again fall silent, with the recent presence of the geese marked by a few white feathers and occasional eggs dropped by females unable to retard their reproductive processes any longer. A million geese are on the last leg of their journey to arctic rendezvous points that are beginning to stir from the bitter memories of winter.[5]

Long ago when the feathered stems were being made, the holy man who was preparing these sacred objects had a dream. In his vision the duck with the green neck appeared and said to him:

"I desire to have a place upon the feathered stem, for I have power to help the Children. This is my power: I lay my eggs near the water and, when the young are hatched, straightway they can swim; the water can not [sic] kill them. When they are grown they can go, flying through the air, from one part of the earth to the other. No place is strange to them; they never lose their way; they can travel over the water without harm and reach safely their destination. They can walk upon the land and find the springs and streams. I am an unerring guide. I know all paths below on the earth, and on the water and above in the air. Put me on the feathered stem where it is grasped by the hand, that the Children may take hold of me and not go astray."

—Pawnee Hako Ceremony[6]

Toward the Rim of the Visible World

Heaven is a great land. In that land there are many holes. These holes we call stars. In the land of heaven lives pan·a (the woman up there) or tap·azuma inua (the one that rules over, or owns, what is up there). There is a mighty spirit, and the anatkut hold that it is a woman. To her pass the souls of the dead. And sometimes, when many die, there are people up there. When anything is spilt up there, it pours out through the stars and becomes rain or snow. The souls of the dead are re-born in the dwellings of pan·a, and brought down to earth again by the moon. When the moon is absent, and cannot be seen in the sky, it is because it is busy helping pan·a by bringing souls to earth. Some become human beings once more, others become animals, all manner of beasts. And so life goes on without end. . . .

—Padlermiut legend[1]

FROM NEAR THE mouth of the Nelson River, northward along the west coast of Hudson Bay, and extending farther into the interior to the north of the Manitoba-Keewatin boundary, the Barren Grounds of Canada stretch away in unbroken solitude to the limits of the arctic coastline. The Chipewyan Indians rarely ventured northward beyond the limits of the coniferous forest; the tundra was the land of their traditional enemies, the Eskimos. It is lifeless in winter, save for ptarmigan, arctic hares, an occasional herd of musk oxen, and such predators as arctic foxes and wolves. Yet in summer it once was invaded by vast herds of caribou that wintered farther south in the wooded areas near the Churchill River (Kogjuaq, or "Big River"). It was also the ancestral home of the Caribou Eskimos. The culture, legends, and survival of these Eskimos of southern Keewatin, the Padlermiut ("People of the Willow Thicket") was more closely linked to the caribou than that of almost any other Eskimo group. Their year was divided into moons that for the most part linked to caribou movements and activities. For the long and bitterly cold period that the caribou were in the forests to the south, the moons of the Padlermiut were nameless, and their only concern was survival.

The annual migration of caribou begins in April, when the cows carrying young start northward toward the tundra, but it is not until early May that the migration is well underway, and many immature animals are on the move. This period was called the Moon in Which the Caribou Go Down. A few late animals, mostly young bulls, are still on the move in early June, the Divided Moon, when both snow-covered and snow-free land is to be seen. However, the adult bulls do not arrive on the northern breeding grounds until August, at about the time of most mating. This was the Moon in Which the Caribou Come. It was in autumn that the greatest caribou hunts always occurred; at that time the animals were in enormous herds, and could be readily approached. It is easy to understand the Eskimo belief that such great numbers of caribou must once have been especially created for them:

Once upon a time there were no caribou on the earth. But then there was a man who wished for caribou, and he cut a great hole deep into the ground, and up through this hole came caribou, many caribou. The caribou came pouring out, till the earth was almost covered with them. And when the man thought there were caribou enough for mankind, he closed up the hole again. Thus the caribou came up on earth.[2]

After the caribou had retreated to the woodlands for the winter, life for the Padlermiut became extremely rigorous, with subzero temperatures to endure and little to eat. Superstitious fears of entering the alien forest prevented them from following the caribou to their wintering grounds. Dried caribou meat was eaten for as long as it lasted, but eventually that would be used up, and it might become necessary to go out and hunt for ptarmigan with bow and arrow in the half-light of the arctic winter.

For the interior Padlermiut, the late-winter period between March and April was always critical. If they did not have enough meat stored in frozen caches, they might starve before the first caribou arrived in May. May was the season of annual rebirth for the Caribou Eskimos and was considered by them to be the start of the year. This situation lasted until the early 1920s, when the Padlermiut were intensively studied by Kaj Birket-Smith and Knud Rasmussen. Dr. Birket-Smith estimated that at the time of his study the total population of Caribou Eskimos was no more than 500 persons. The two largest units were an interior group centered on Lake Yathkyed, and a coastal population near Eskimo Point, each of which numbered about a hundred persons.[3]

In the late 1940s the interior Caribou Eskimos were revisited by Farley Mowat, who located a small colony of these people still surviving between Lake Yathkyed and Lake Ennadai. In this area of low hills, within the general range of the Padlermiut, the Eskimos he found called themselves the Ihalmiut ("the People of the Little Hills"). Famine and disease had badly thinned their ranks since the time of Rasmussen and Birket-Smith. The caribou their lives depended upon had been slaughtered by the tens of thousands on their wintering grounds by the Indians, whose hunts had been facilitated by the availability of repeating rifles. Famine during the late winter of 1949–50 further decimated the remaining Ihalmiut, and by spring of 1950 their population numbered about 30 individuals. Mowat later reported that by 1958 the total population of Ihalmiut consisted of some 60 people, the majority of whom then were living at Rankin Inlet.[4]

The coastal group of Caribou Eskimos has long been con-

centrated in the vicinity of Eskimo Point (Tikerarjualag, or
"The Long Forefinger"), one of several narrow, sandy eskers
that extend several miles out into Hudson Bay. Rasmussen
considered them to comprise a distinct group, the Padlimiut, or
"the People of the River Mouth out by the Sea."

Because of their proximity to the sea these coastal people were
not quite so tightly bound to the caribou as were the more interior groups, although caribou meat was still their primary food.
However, they supplemented it with seal and walrus meat, as
well as with sea trout and other fish. They also collected goose
eggs in late June from the colonies of snow geese and Canada
geese nesting nearby. Further, because of their much more frequent contacts with white traders, the coastal Eskimos eventually
acquired modern rifles with which to hunt, and soon learned
to trade fox fur for such staples as flour, lard, and tea. In contrast to the dismal condition of the interior Caribou Eskimos, the
population in the vicinity of the coast has continued to thrive,
and at present Eskimo Point even is served by regular commer-
cial air flights from Churchill.[5]

Not far to the north of Eskimo Point the exposed rocks of
the Canadian Shield extend to the shoreline of Hudson Bay, producing a rocky and highly indented coastline. To the south, the
coastline is a low and flat sedimentary plain that merges with the
sea and has many braided streams and marshy lowlands along
the coast. A narrow band of tundralike vegetation extends
along this coastline almost to the Nelson River, with the trees
gradually coming closer to the shore as one progresses southward, and with the forest becoming more luxuriant. In late May,
Canada geese and pintails join the flocks of elders and oldsquaws that are rafting along the icy edges and leads of open
water. The calls of the oldsquaws drift in across the bay and
merge with the raucous cry of male ptarmigans moving from
their forested wintering areas into breeding territories on the
open tundra.

The snow geese normally arrive in the Eskimo Point region
during the last week of May, probably after having flown in
directly from their last stopover point near the mouth of the

Nelson River about 300 miles to the south. For the birds that are destined to breed on Southampton Island, Eskimo Point represents the last suitable resting place prior to their crossing of Hudson Bay, since the rocky coastline to the north is lacking in suitable foraging areas.

On the first day of June, Khavik and his two offspring arrive at the mouth of the McConnell River, 20 miles south of Eskimo Point. They left the delta of the Nelson River during the early morning hours and, since daylight in early June lasts for 18 hours at this latitude, have reached the McConnell River well before midday. Thousands of snow geese have preceded them and many have already begun their nesting activities. The earliest have begun to deposit eggs in nest scrapes on the large island at the river's mouth. The small Canada geese breeding in the same area are a few days behind the snow geese in their reproductive cycles, but soon will begin laying eggs. They have followed a very similar migratory route northward from their wintering grounds along the Gulf Coast of Mexico and Texas as have the lesser snow geese. Like them, many of the small Canada geese at McConnell River are not yet home, but will go to more northerly breeding grounds along the coasts of Keewatin, Baffin, and Southampton islands.[6]

The snow geese that are headed for breeding grounds on Southampton Island are restless, in spite of having just arrived at McConnell River. Behind them lie nine months of exile from their nesting grounds, and a round-trip migration route of nearly 5,000 miles. Ahead there is a short flight across the frozen flats of Hudson Bay to the nearest landfall of Southampton. The birds occasionally rest and forage in the rays of the late afternoon sun. Yet, they are nervous, and their feeding activities are erratic and half-hearted. As the warm afternoon wears on toward a cool evening, there is a rising murmur that moves across the flock like ripples on a pond. The birds stretch their necks and scan the sky, as if searching for some kind of signal. In the northwest, a reddening sun hangs low over the distant horizon. Somewhat beyond, a few caribou are still plodding northward, and even fewer People of the Caribou are still lying in wait for them. It is a re-enactment of an ancient story; for as long as any caribou remain to be hunted, and there are People to hunt them, it will be so.

As the sun is about to touch the distant horizon, flock after flock of geese begins to take wing amid a chorus of calls. The rays of the sun strike their white undersides, painting them with delicate shades of pink. As the birds gain altitude, the sun momentarily seems to rise, flaring like a distant campfire from the Time that Used to Be. Then the birds level off and unhesitatingly set their course northeastward toward the rim of the visible world. Soon they are out of sight, and in the slowly darkening skies the only evidence of their presence is the echo of goose music resounding over the frozen sea. Those who know no better might think it is only the calls of the departing birds, but the People know that it is the laughter of the goose-gods, rejoicing in the annual return of their kind.

May their roads home be on the trail of peace,
Happily may they all return.
In beauty I walk,
With beauty before me, I walk,
With beauty behind me, I walk,
With beauty above and about me, I walk.
It is finished in beauty.
It is finished in beauty.

—Navaho Night Chant[7]

Twenty-seven
Photographs
by the author

Snow geese arriving at breeding grounds.
Old squaw male in summer.
Eiders on Hudson Bay. (Page 114)
Nearly every boulder supports a herring gull nest. (Page 115)

Female khanguk. (left)
Male khavik. (right)

*Two snow geese and one newly
hatched snow-phase gosling* (Page *119*)

Two snow geese. LEFT: *one pipping egg;*
RIGHT: *a newly hatched snow-phase gosling.*
Khavik with a blue-phase gosling. (opposite)
Fall stopover point, western Iowa. (Page 122)
A fall flock of migrating geese. (Page 123)

Winter concentration of snow geese.
Grazing snow goose.

Bibliographic Notes

CHAPTER 1

1. The effects of the last glaciation on distribution patterns and resulting speciation in arctic waterfowl has been discussed by P. L. Ploeger, "Geographical differentiation in Arctic Anatidae as a result of isolation during the last glacial." *Ardea*, 56:1–159, 1968.

2. See account by J. A. Elson, "Geology of Glacial Lake Agassiz," in: *Life, Land and Water*. University of Manitoba Press, Winnipeg, 1967.

3. Based on work of C. T. Shay, "Vegetation history of the southern Lake Agassiz Basin during the past 12,000 years," pp. 231–52, in: *Life, Land and Water*. University of Manitoba Press, Winnipeg, 1967.

4. For details on these sites, see W. J. Mayer-Oaks, "Prehistoric human population history of the Glacial Lake Agassiz region," pp. 339–78, in: *Life, Land and Water*. University of Manitoba Press, Winnipeg, 1967.

5. See discussion by D. L. Allen, *The Life of Prairies and Plains*. McGraw-Hill Book Co., New York, 1967.

6. From F. Boas, "The Eskimos of Baffin Land and Hudson Bay." *Bulletin of the American Museum of Natural History*, Vol. 15, 1907.

7. G. M. Sutton, "The blue goose and lesser snow goose on Southampton Island, Hudson Bay." *Auk*, 48:335–64, 1931.

8. T. H. Manning, "Blue and lesser snow geese on Southampton and Baffin islands." *Auk*, 59:158–75.

9. F. G. Cooch, "Ecological aspects of the blue-snow goose complex." *Auk*, 78:72–79, 1961.

10. For details, see F. Cooke and P. J. Mirsky, "A genetic analysis of lesser snow goose families." *Auk*, 89:863–71, 1972. Also see F. Cooke, P. J. Mirsky, and M. B. Seiger, "Color preference in the lesser snow goose and their possible role in mate selection." *Canadian Journal of Zoology*, 50:529–636, 1972.

CHAPTER 2

1. See F. G. Cooch, op. cit.

2. J. D. Soper, "Life history of the blue goose, *Chen caerulescens* (Linnaeus)." *Proceedings of the Boston Society of Natural History*, 42:125–222, 1943.

3. See F. G. Cooch, op. cit.

4. T. W. Barry, "Geese of the Anderson River Delta, Northwest Territories, Canada." Unpublished Ph.D. dissertation, University of Alberta, Edmonton.

5. S. M. Uspenski, "The geese of Wrangel Island," pp. 126–29. *16th Annual Report of the Wildfowl Trust*, 1965.

6. F. Salomonsen, "The moult migration," pp. 5–24, *Wildfowl* 19:5–24, 1968.

7. The Eskimo names given here are for the most part those listed for Southampton Island by G. M. Sutton, in "The birds of Southampton Island." Memoirs of the Carnegie Museum, 12 (part 2, section 2), 1932.

8. See F. Boas, op. cit.

9. K. Rasmussen, "Observations on the intellectual culture of the Caribou Eskimos." *Report of the Fifth Thule Expedition*, 1921–24, Vol. 7, No. 2. Gyldendalske Boghandel, Nordisk Forlag, Copenhagen, 1930.

10. D. Jenness, "Myths and traditions from northern Alaska, the Mackenzie Delta and Coronation Gulf." Report of the Canadian Arctic Expedition, 1913–18, Vol. XIII, 1924.

11. From S. C. Simms, "Myths of the Bungees or Swampy Indians of Lake Winnipeg." *Journal of American Folk-lore*, 19:334–40, 1906.

CHAPTER 3

1. See J. M. Harvey, "Factors affecting blue goose nesting success." *Canadian Journal of Zoology*, 49:223–34, 1971.

2. See F. G. Cooch, op. cit.

3. F. G. Cooch, "The breeding biology and management of the blue goose, *Chen caerulescens*." Ph.D. dissertation, Cornell University, Ithaca, New York, 1958.

4. See T. H. Manning, op. cit.

5. F. G. Cooch, "Mass ringing of flightless blue and lesser snow geese in Canada's eastern Arctic," pp. 58–67, in *8th Annual Report of the Wildfowl Trust*, 1957.

6. W. Jones, "Ojibwa Texts." *Publications of the American Ethnological Society*, Vol. VII, part 1, 501 pp., 1917.

7. From A. C. Fletcher, "The Hako: A Pawnee ceremonial." *22nd Annual Report of the Bureau of American Ethnology*, Smithsonian Institution, part 2, 1903.

CHAPTER 4

1. As a result of the James Bay Hydroelectric Project, two reservoirs inundating 3,400 and 1,700 square miles will soon be impounded and may eventually destroy the present ecology of James Bay. See Boyce Richardson, *James Bay: The Plot to Drown the North Woods*. Sierra Club, San Francisco, 1972.

2. J. R. Jehl, Jr., and B. A. Smith, "Birds of the Churchill region, Manitoba." *Special Publication No. 1*, Manitoba Museum of Man and Nature, Winnipeg, 1970. By 1972 this colony had reached about 2,500 nesting pairs.

3. This colony was first described by H. G. Lumsden, "A snow goose breeding colony in Ontario." *Canadian Field-Naturalist*, 71:153–54, 1957. It has continued to grow since that time, and now is the second largest colony on the coastline of Hudson Bay as well as the southernmost ("Birds of the Cape Henrietta Maria region, Ontario." *Canadian Field-Naturalist*, 86:333–48, 1972). Recent unpublished U. S. Fish and Wildlife Service estimates of fall lesser snow goose populations from each of the major eastern Canadian breeding colonies are: Queen Maud Gulf, 40,000; Baffin Island, 1,210,000; Southampton Island, 190,000; McConnell River, 500,000; La Pérouse Bay, 10,000; Cape Hen-

rietta Maria, 120,000. These figures suggest a total eastern Canada fall population of over two million birds, or almost twice as many as the highest of recent midwinter estimates.

4. The descriptions of James Bay, its vegetation, and the snow goose harvest estimates are based on the account by G. M. Stirrett, "Field observations of geese in James Bay, with special reference to the blue goose." *Transactions of the 19th North American Wildlife Conference*, pp. 211–20, 1954. More recent (1969 and 1970 seasons) estimates of the retrieved kill of lesser snow geese for Ontario and Manitoba indicate about 28,000 geese are shot by sportsmen in these two provinces annually, for a total Canadian harvest (including Indian hunters) of about 100,000 birds. The estimates of the U.S. harvests for the Mississippi and Central Flyways flocks for the 1966 through 1969 seasons indicate an average annual retrieved kill of about 257,000 geese, or a total retrieved kill of some 357,000 geese from the Hudson Bay population per year. December inventories of this population for the same period averaged 671,000 birds which, together with the estimated hunter harvest, would indicate a minimum fall population of 1,028,000 geese, and a harvest rate of 37.7 per cent. Although it does not take into account unretrieved kills or non-hunting losses, this figure is quite close to the annual 37 per cent adult mortality rate that has been estimated for this population by Hugh Boyd (citation ※10, Chapter 8). During the period 1950 to 1971 the winter surveys of these geese have indicated that the proportion of juvenile birds in these flocks averaged 30.25 per cent over the entire period, with annual variations from 6.0 to 54.2 per cent. (J. J. Lynch, "Productivity and Morality among Geese, Swans and Brant," 1971 Annual Report, Lafayette Station, Bureau of Sport Fisheries and Wildlife.) These figures would suggest that the goose population is presently being harvested at a rate equal to or exceeding its average annual productivity.

5. J. R. Forster, "An account of the birds sent from Hudson's Bay; with observations relative to their natural history; and Latin descriptions of some of the most common." *Philosophical Transactions of the Royal Society of London*, Vol. 62, p. 382, 1771.

6. See F. G. Cooch, "Observations on the autumn migration of blue geese." *Wilson Bulletin*, 67:171–74, 1955.

7. The ecology and geology of these potholes have been discussed by H. A. Hochbaum, "Contemporary drainage within true prairie of the glacial Lake Agassiz Basin," pp. 197–203, in: *Life, Land and Water*, University of Manitoba Press, Winnipeg, 1967. Many of these marshes in the Devils Lake area are destined for destruction by the Starkweather Drainage Project, which for incomprehensible reasons the U. S. Fish and Wildlife Service recently approved after being awarded control of certain wetland areas in exchange. Other marshes, such as Johns Lake in Sheridan County, have already been destroyed by the Bureau of Reclamation's Garrison Diversion Project, which threatens to be both an ecological and economic disaster. (R. Madson, "Rumblings on the Ditch," *North Dakota Union Farmer*, Vol. 18, No. 10, July 1972.)

8. W. Jones, op. cit.

CHAPTER 5

1. H. Alexander, *North American Mythology*. Marshall Jones Co., Boston, 1916.

2. This description of the pristine James River (originally called the Jacques or Dakota River) is in sharp contrast to its present condition, as described by

R. Madson in "Prairie river: Heritage threatened," *North Dakota Union Farmer,* Vol. 17, No. 10, July 1971. During a spring canoe trip down the river from its source near Bowdon to its confluence with the Missouri near Yankton, South Dakota, Madson found 158 dead animals floating in the river or on its banks, 95 junkpiles, abundant raw sewage, and massive accumulations of silt deposits reflecting poor soil-conservation practices along its 796-mile length. If this degradation of the river were not enough, the U. S. Corps of Engineers now has plans to channelize the river from Jamestown to Yankton in order to make it suitable for barge traffic. Thus the river is threatened both at its upper end, by the Garrison Diversion Project, and by channelization plans for its lower portions. Within a few years one of North Dakota's most beautiful rivers is likely to be permanently destroyed.

3. This account of Sand Lake and the goose-hunting practices there has been primarily based on the shocking article by G. Sherwood, "Carnage at Sand Lake." *Audubon,* Vol. 72, No. 6, pp. 66–73, 1970. Since the publication of his article, some management changes for the better have been instituted, but the goose slaughter still continues almost unabated. Estimated snow and blue goose harvests in the refuge area for the 1970 and 1971 season were 19,415 and 28,879 respectively.

4. From J. G. Neihardt, *Black Elk Speaks.* William Morrow Co., 1932. It was a chance reading of this book, at a time when I was reviewing the technical literature on snow goose biology in conjunction with another writing project, that made me aware of the great gulf between the Indian's view of animals and nature and the current attitude of our federal agencies to the effect that waterfowl are simply objects of recreational use, to be harvested as fully as the populations allow. I thus resolved to try to write a story that not only might be biologically accurate, but which might also bring into sharp focus the contrasting visions of our natural resources as seen by aboriginal North Americans and by our policy-making bureaucrats in Washington, as well as establish parallels in the attitudes of whites toward both our wildlife and the Indians.

CHAPTER 6

1. J. G. Neihardt, *Black Elk Speaks.* William Morrow Co., 1932.

2. R. D. Burroughs, *The Natural History of the Lewis and Clark Expedition.* Michigan State University Press, East Lansing, 1961.

3. Information provided by James Salyer, Refuge Manager, DeSoto Bend National Wildlife Refuge.

4. E. W. Nelson, "The Eskimos about Bering Strait." *18th Annual Report of the Bureau of American Ethnology,* Smithsonian Institution, part 1, pp. 1–518, 1896–97.

CHAPTER 7

1. Information provided by Harold Burgess, Refuge Manager, Squaw Creek National Wildlife Refuge.

2. M. R. Gilmore, *Prairie Smoke,* Bismarck, N.D., published by the author, 1922.

CHAPTER 8

1. The information on the Texas coastal wintering areas was derived from R. J. Buller, "Central Flyway," pp. 209–32, in: *Waterfowl Tomorrow*, U. S. Department of Interior, Government Printing Office, Washington, D.C., 1964.

2. V. W. Lehmann, "Attwater's prairie chicken; its life history and management." U. S. Department of Interior, Fish and Wildlife Service. *North American Fauna No. 67*, 66 pp., 1941.

3. E. E. Horn and L. L. Glasgow, "Rice and waterfowl," pp. 435–43, in: *Waterfowl Tomorrow*, U. S. Department of Interior, Government Printing Office, Washington, D.C., 1964.

4. W. C. Glazener, "Food habits of wild geese on the Gulf Coast of Texas." *Journal of Wildlife Management*, 10:322–29, 1946.

5. E. A. McIlhenney, "The blue goose in its winter home." *Auk*, 49:279–306, 1932.

6. J. J. Lynch, "Values of the South Atlantic and Gulf Coast marshes and estuaries to waterfowl," pp. 51–63, in: *Proceedings of the Marsh and Estuary Symposium, Louisiana State University*, Baton Rouge, 1968.

7. F. C. Bellrose, "Waterfowl migration corridors east of the Rocky Mountains of the United States." *Biological Notes No. 61*, Illinois Natural History Survey, June 1968.

8. R. M. Nowak, "The mysterious wolf of the South." *Natural History*, Vol. 81, No. 1, pp. 50–53, 74–77, 1971.

9. Based on observations by F. G. Cooch (citation ⚡3, Chapter 3) and P. A. Johnsgard, *Handbook of Waterfowl Behavior*, Comstock Press, Ithaca, New York, 1965.

10. H. Boyd, "Population dynamics and the exploitation of ducks and geese," pp. 85–95, in: *The Exploitation of Natural Animal Populations*. John Wiley & Sons, New York, 1962. The west coast data are from W. C. Reinecker, "A summary of band returns from lesser snow geese (*Chen hyperborea*) of the Pacific Flyway." *California Fish and Game*, 51:132–46, 196.

11. C. D. Stutzenbaker, "Distribution dilemma." *Texas Parks and Wildlife*, Vol. 28, No. 12, pp. 12–14. December 1970. See also H. Bateman, "Blue and snow geese short-stopping." *Louisiana Conservationist*, 23 (1 & 2):4–9, January, February 1971.

12. D. I. Bushnell, Jr., "Myths of the Louisiana Choctaw." *American Anthropologist*, n. s., Vol. 12, pp. 526–35, 1910. Reproduced by permission of the Anthropological Association from the *American Anthropologist*.

CHAPTER 9

1. F. LaFlesche, "The Osage Tribe." *36th Annual Report of the Bureau of American Ethnology*, Smithsonian Institution, 604 pp., 1914–15.

2. A review of the geology of the Nebraska sandhills may be found in C. B. Schultz and J. C. Frey (eds.), *Loess and Related Aeolian Deposits of the World*, University of Nebraska Press, Lincoln, 1968. The role of rainwater basin in providing waterfowl production habitat has been discussed by R. D. Evans and C. W. Wolfe, Jr., "Waterfowl production in the Rainwater Basin area of Nebraska." *Journal of Wildlife Management*, 31:788–94, 1967.

3. The status of the Mid-State Project presently (1973) depends on the re-

sults of an environmental impact study and the subscription of enough farmers for use of irrigation waters in order to allow the planners to proceed with congressional requests for construction funds. However, increasing opposition by private, state, and national environmental organizations may further delay or prevent its construction.

4. F. LaFlesche, "War ceremony and peace ceremony of the Osage Indian." *Bulletin of the Bureau of American Ethnology*, Smithsonian Institution, 101:1–230, 1939.

CHAPTER 10

1. R. B. Dixon, "Maidu texts." *Publications of the American Ethnological Society*, 4:1–241, 1912.

2. C. L. Matsch and H. E. Wright, Jr., "The southern outlet of Lake Agassiz," pp. 121–40, in: *Life, Land and Water*, University of Manitoba Press, Winnipeg, 1967.

3. W. J. Sladen and W. W. Cochran, "Studies of the whistling swan, 1967–1969." *Transactions of the North American Wildlife and Natural Resources Conference*, 34:42–50, 1969.

4. The Thunder Bird legend and information on pictographic rocks is from W. H. Over, "Indian picture writing in South Dakota." University of South Dakota Museum, Archaeological Studies, Circular IV, 59 pp., 1941.

5. This description of the spring departure is based on H. Blockpoel "Observations on the spring migration of lesser snow and blue geese through southern Manitoba." Field Note No. 56, Association Committee on Bird Hazards to Aircraft, National Research Council, Ottawa, Canada. 14 pp. (mimeo), 1971.

6. See A. C. Fletcher, op. cit.

CHAPTER 11

1. K. Rasmussen, op. cit.

2. Ibid.

3. K. Birket-Smith, "The Caribou Eskimo. Material and social life and their cultural position," *Report of the Fifth Thule Expedition*, 1921–24, Vol. 5, Gyldendalske Boghandel, Nordisk Forlag, Copenhagen, 1929.

4. F. Mowat, *People of the Deer*, 1951, and *The Desperate People*, 1959. Little, Brown & Company, Boston.

5. D. B. Marsh, "Canada's Caribou Eskimos." *National Geographic*, 91 (1): 87–104, 1947.

6. The breeding biology of the Canada geese nesting at the McConnell River has been studied by C. D. MacInnes, "Nesting of small Canada geese near Eskimo Point, Northwest Territories," *Journal of Wildlife Management*, 26:247–56, 1962.

7. W. Matthews, "The Night Chant, a Navaho Ceremony," *American Museum of Natural History Memoirs*, No. 6, 1902.

Acknowledgments

IT IS EXTREMELY difficult to acknowledge fully the help I have received in writing a book that was so long in its philosophic development, even though the actual writing occurred over a period of only a few months. Were it not for the emotional stimulus provided by my reading of *Black Elk Speaks*, by J. G. Neihardt, I probably would not have delved into the older Eskimo and Indian literature, which has influenced so greatly the story that I have tried to develop. Even though most of the persons who recounted, transcribed, or published these ethnological materials are long since deceased, I would be greatly remiss if I were not to acknowledge their help.

Once I committed myself to writing the story, I obtained advice and information from many persons, prominent among them being Harold Burgess, Russel Clapper, and James Salyer, refuge managers of Squaw Creek, Anahuac, and DeSoto National Wildlife Refuges respectively. Other state, federal, or provincial biologists who assisted me in various ways included Loren Bonde, Richard Kerbes, John Lynch, Charles Schroeder, George Schildman, and John Walther.

From the outset I believed that the story could best be illustrated by drawings of an interpretive and semimystical type, to reflect the symbolic attitudes of the aboriginal Americans toward their environment. I was thus especially gratified when Paul Geraghty agreed to provide these illustrations, since in my opinion his visual interpretations of nature somehow capture the essence of this special feeling for the natural world.

Although it was not possible to observe personally the Southampton Island nesting grounds described in the text, I was able to visit the snow goose breeding colony at La Pérouse Bay, which is currently under study by Dr. Fred Cooke and his associates. The great help and hospitality of Dr. Cooke, Dr. John Ryder, and the other "goose camp" personnel provided some of the most memorable and enjoyable moments of the entire project. Similarly, Des and Jen Bartlett were congenial hosts at their photographic camp and shared with me their great love and enthusiasm for the snow geese. Further, Mr. and Mrs. Robert Montgomerie immeasurably assisted me during my summer work in the Churchill area. Lastly, I owe a special debt of gratitude to Brother Jacques Volant, O.M.I., curator of the Eskimo Museum at Churchill, for his kindness in letting me examine and photograph some of the items in that collection.

For nearly all the typing on the manuscript, and indeed for the very idea that I should try to write a "popular" story rather than a technical monograph, I must thank Janet Olander. Repeated urgings by her and Vicki Peterson, while both were departmental secretaries, finally convinced me that such an effort would be worth undertaking. For Janet's help on content and style, as well as the actual job of retyping my rough drafts, I offer my sincere thanks. Parts or all of the manuscript were read and criticized by several people, including Harold Burgess, Russel Clapper, H. A. Hochbaum, Mary Lou Pritchard, and James Salyer, whose suggestions were invariably appreciated even if they were not always followed. I thus take the entire responsibility for the materials presented here.

Index

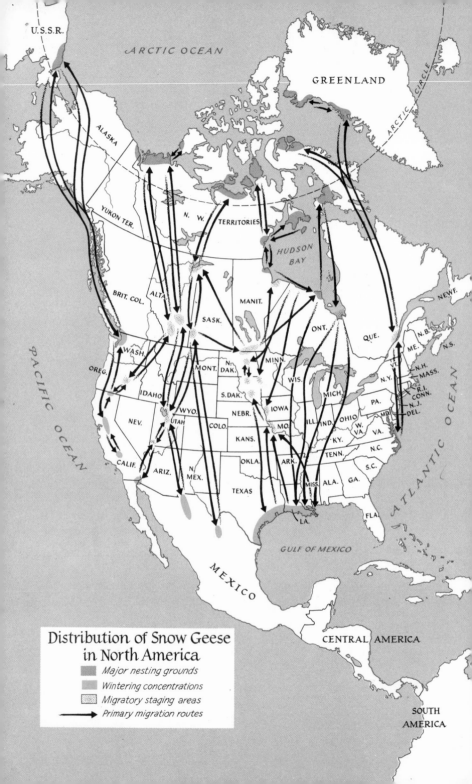

Distribution of Snow Geese
in North America

Major nesting grounds
Wintering concentrations
Migratory staging areas
Primary migration routes